CLAVES
INTELLIGENTIARUM

CLAVES INTELLIGENTIARUM:
A COMPLETE MANUAL OF CONJURATION OF THE PLANETARY INTELLIGENCES
Copyright © 2024 David Rankine
Redrawn manuscript images © Rosa Laguna.
All Rights Reserved.

ISBN 978-1-915933-67-6 (Hardcover)
ISBN 978-1-915933-68-3 (Softcover)

A CIP catalogue for this title is available from the British Library.
10 9 8 7 6 5 4 3 2 1

Except in the case of quotations embedded in critical articles or reviews, no part of this book may be reproduced or transmitted in any form or by any means, electronic or mechanical, including photocopying, recording, or by any information storage and retrieval system, without permission in writing from the publisher.

David Rankine has asserted his moral right to be identified as the author of this work.

Published in 2024
Hadean Press
West Yorkshire
England

www.hadeanpress.com

CLAVES INTELLIGENTIARUM

A COMPLETE PRACTICAL MANUAL OF CONJURATION OF THE PLANETARY INTELLIGENCES

DAVID RANKINE

This book is dedicated to:

Jason Miller, whose words inspired me to write this book, and whose books and courses inspire all who engage with them.

Stephen Skinner, whose hugely important work *Techniques of High Magic* started me on my path of practice back in 1979, and who has inspired me since then through his excellent and extensive work, our collaborations, and our friendship.

Contents

Acknowledgements ix

Introduction 1

Planning 5

Timings 11

The Tools and their Consecrations 13

Fragrances 28

The Lead-In 30

License to Remain (Optional) 36

The Triangle 38

The Magic Circle 42

Afterword 52

Appendix I: Planetary Days & Hours 53

Appendix II: Sigil Construction Using Aiq Beker 59

Appendix III: Images of the Sigils and Seals 66

Appendix IV: Talisman/Seal/Lamen Construction 74

Appendix V: Archangel Prayers 76

Appendix VI: Planetary Intelligence Conjurations 84

Appendix VII: Shapes Of Spirits 99

Appendix VIII: Dream Charms 101

Bibliography 103

Index 105

ACKNOWLEDGEMENTS

Thanks to my beloved wife Rosa Laguna for the excellent front cover, and being the first person I know of to draw up a complete accurate set of planetary intelligence sigils in history!

Dorian Bones and La Societa' dello Zolfo for inviting me to give lectures and workshops which have proved very inspirational and fruitful for me.

As always, thanks to Erzebet Barthold for being such a great editor, publisher, and friend.

Thanks also to the people who read the draft and offered their valuable insights and comments: Aaman Lamda, Alexander Eth, Andrew Theitic, Jason Miller, Jim Baker, Mat Hadfield, Stephen Skinner, and Steve Savedow.

Books are bound with glory – they bode
Good counsel and conscious will.
They are man's strength and firm foundation,
His anchored thought. They lift the mind
From melancholy and help hard need.
Solomon and Saturn (9th/10th century)

INTRODUCTION

IT IS A CURIOUS SENSATION TO BE AWARE OF THE MOMENT YOUR MIND CREATES the seed of a book you know you need to write. Often it is the collision or friction of ideas and words, generating the excitement and impetus which leads to the work of writing the book. That is the case for this work. I was putting material together for a workshop on conjuring the Planetary Intelligences for an Italian group, the La Societa' dello Zolfo, and Jason Miller's words from a review he wrote of my *Grimoire Encyclopaedia* came to mind: "This is Rankine the Conjuror, a voice that he frankly doesn't speak in often enough."[1]

In that moment I thought of how I often recommend people start their conjuration path by working with the Planetary Intelligences, and that I was offering empty advice without giving them a coherent structure to back this up. I stand by the statement that I think it is an excellent introduction to grimoire conjuring, but until then I was not considering that the grimoires do not give the conjurations of these Intelligences within a framework of practice. It is therefore necessary to provide the framework I have created with compatible techniques to give a complete sequence that facilitates successful conjuration of the Planetary Intelligences.

This work is my attempt to make that advice worthwhile by giving the entire process I have created and used over the years, elaborating on all the steps and qualifying and codifying the material. The result is a manual which is aimed at giving a person who has never performed a conjuration everything they need to know and do to practice it. Of course I hope it will also be of value to people who have practiced conjuration as a comparison which may offer ideas or insights they have not yet had.[2]

For the practice of conjuration, the ideal number of practitioners is at least three. The roles are conjuror, skryer, and scribe. The conjuror, in addition to asking questions, can also act as the scribe, reducing the number to two whilst maintaining an effective balance. While success can be achieved in solitary practice, it is better avoided; maintaining

---

1 https://strategicsorcery.net/what-does-one-do-with-a-grimoire-encyclopedia/

2 Please note I am not suggesting my practice is superior here, but rather that we all have different insights based on our experiences.

the focus required for skrying and spirit contact while asking the questions and recording the answers is not an easy balance to achieve.

So, before beginning the process itself, allow me to clarify the parameters within which this book was written. I recognise the positive value in the development and restructuring of grimoire practice within its ancient Greek goetic roots;[3] however, since I have worked within the traditional framework with the Planetary Intelligences with repeated success, this is how it is presented. Additionally, the Intelligences first appear in the writings of Agrippa, placing them firmly in the Christian cosmology era of the grimoire tradition. I appreciate some people may have issues with the Abrahamic terminology of the divine names due to personal experiences or traumas in their pasts, but this is the way the grimoire tradition developed. Consequently I would not recommend swapping them out with pagan alternatives as this may result in these conjurations failing. The Intelligences operate within a specific hierarchy that pagan deities are not a part of. It is worth remembering that many of the divine names are actually *titles* for the divine if this helps.

I acknowledge that there are elements in my practice which have been influenced by more recent ceremonial magic, such as the use of visualisation in the circle consecration.[4] I have updated the language used in consecrations, conjurations, etc., to reflect our time period and make the flow easier to recite. The exception to this is the words Thou/Thee/Thy/Thine, which I feel add a certain gravitas by their use. I have also made changes on occasion which reflect the use of more modern materials, as magic takes on the technology of the age, and evolves, making this a logical development.

As there were no sources for the complete process of conjuration of the Intelligences, I synthesised what I felt was the most appropriate material from other Solomonic grimoires.[5] I also included components that I use for all my conjurations that have demonstrated their efficacy in contributing to successful conjuration in over forty years of practice. I will

---

3 As inspired by the work of the late, great Jake Stratton-Kent and carried on by many others today.

4 This is how I was taught, and whilst it is not traditional grimoire practice, it is very effective and I have continued with it for this reason.

5 Note that for anyone who complains that this bit from the *Key of Solomon* is missing, or that I changed the words on that bit: I repeat, this is a synthesis I have created. The material is all here because it has worked successfully on numerous occasions. *Probatim est.*

list the sources of all the different components so the process of synthesis is clear. With grimoire practice some things change and others do not, as Frank Klaasen wrote of the author of the *Boxgrove Manual* (circa 1600):

> Like his forebears in the traditions of ritual magic he sought to discover and construct a true, good, and coherent practice of magic from sources that were not systematically unified. Also like them, the magic he made was an idiosyncratic synthesis.[6]

David Rankine
June 2024, Alcalá de Guadaíra, Spain

---

6 Klaasen, 2019:85.

PLANNING

ONE OF THE FIRST THINGS TO DO WHEN DECIDING TO PERFORM A CONJURATION is to find out everything you can about the spirit you intend to conjure. The earliest reference to the Planetary Intelligences by name comes in Agrippa's *Three Books of Occult Philosophy*, making this the primary source, although only for their names as their offices (specific roles) are not given. They are also found collectively in the *Key of Solomon* (Rabbi Solomon text family), *Boxgrove Manual*, Sloane 3821, *Pneumatologia Occulta*, and *The Magus*. Of these the *Key of Solomon*, *Boxgrove Manual*, and *Pneumatologia Occulta* repeat the names and seals from Agrippa but offer no other information.[7] *The Magus* is also heavily derivative of Agrippa and offers no additional information.

Some of the Intelligences also appear individually in other grimoires, so these are worth checking to see what they may add. Tiriel and Malcha are mentioned in a charm in the *Grimoire of Pope Honorius* which is also found in *Grimorium Verum*, but only as part of a list of spirits in a charm to make a woman seek you even if she is not inclined.[8] *A Cunning Man's Grimoire* has a working for an oracle or true dream using a Mercurial kamea with Tiriel.[9] I was very pleased to find this, as I had extrapolated the same technique previously, deriving it from a later French text for angelic dream contact.[10] This is included in Appendix VIII and may be used as part of the preparation to improve the contact and increase the magical momentum of the conjuration. It is strongly recommended, especially for the skryer, but all participants will benefit from doing it.

Descriptions of their offices and a series of conjurations of the Intelligences is found in the manuscript Sloane 3821, which I published as *Conjuring the Planetary Intelligences* (2018). This makes it the main information source, and provides the actual conjurations used in this work. This text

---

7 Although the *Boxgrove Manual* does include several seals which include the Intelligences, and several seals of Hagiel, they are not given with conjurations, and I have not worked with them. For this reason I have not included them in this work due to the lack of relevance to the sequence I am giving.

8 Peterson, 2007:47.

9 Skinner & Rankine, 2018:122-23.

10 *A Collection of Magical Secrets*. Rankine, 2009:123-133.

begins with a description of the Planetary Intelligences which I include for its interesting description of them:

> Referred to the seven planets and those Notes or Magical figures which have called the labels of the planets and also are endowed with many & very great virtues of the honours inasmuch as they represent that Divine order of Celestial Numbers impressed upon Celestials by the Ideas of the Divine Mind by means of the soul of the world by the sweet harmony of the Celestial Rays Signifying according to the proposition of Euclid[11] Superior Celestial Intelligences which can no other way be expressed thereby by the Maker of Numbers & Characters for Material Numbers & figures can it do nothing in the mysteries of his things but Represent hereby by formal Numbers & figures as they are governed & Informed by Intelligences & Divine Numerations which unite the Elements of the matter & Spirit to the will of the Elevated soul honouring through great affection by the Celestial power of the judicious practitioner in sublime Aid & power from God supplied through the soul of the universe & observations of Celestial Constellations to a matter fit for Affecting the medium being disposed by the skill and industry of the sober & just prophecies.[12]

Sloane 3821 describes the Intelligences as being courteous, benevolent and affable on appearance. I have also found this to be the case: they are definitely some of the most easy-going spirits to work with. I have supplemented the recorded qualities given for each Intelligence with other possible qualities based on contemporary texts, so you can decide which Intelligence is the one you wish to work with for the results you are after.

Although Agrippa is the first to record the Planetary Intelligences in the grimoires, the notion of Intelligences as spirits goes back to the ancient world. The Greek Neoplatonist philosopher Proclus (412-485 CE), in his discussion of Intelligences, stated. 'Every intelligence has its existence, its potency and its activity in eternity. For if every intelligence has its existence established in eternity, and with its existence its activity, each

---

11 Euclid, the 'father of geometry', who lived mid-4th – mid-3rd century BCE.
12 Sloane 3821 fo 226.

one will know all [relevant] things simultaneously.'[13] This gives an early clarification of why you would want to conjure a Planetary Intelligence.

AGIEL – INTELLIGENCE OF SATURN

Qualities of Agiel are listed in Sloane 3821 as:
- Good in helping with childbirth, making it safe and less stressful for mother and child, as well as preventing miscarriage.
- Making a person safe and powerful.
- Giving good success in petitions and addresses to powerful people and government powers.[14]

Other qualities associated with Saturn that could be considered are:[15]
- Contemplation, resolution, understanding.
- Strengthening self-discipline.
- Issues with time. Also matters relating to history.
- Improving practicality.

JOHPHIEL/JOPHIEL – INTELLIGENCE OF JUPITER

Qualities of Johphiel are listed in Sloane 3821 as:
- Good in assisting to gain and enjoy the favour and agreement of powerful people.
- Good to appease enemies.
- Good for gaining honours and dignities.
- To reveal enchantments.
- To control autocratic people and those who do not treat their subordinates well, forcing them to submit.

Other qualities associated with Jupiter that could be considered are:
- Developing faith and piety.
- Improving modesty in a person.

---

13 Proclus, 1963:47, 149.

14 I am updating references to royalty into more modern terms appropriate to today. Additionally some of the other qualities, such as to see or be contacted by a person within half an hour, may be seen in a different way in our modern age of mobiles, emails, and video calls, etc.

15 Note the additional attributions I am including are drawn from grimoires like *Janua Magica Reserata*, not modern magical or astrological texts.

- Developing grace and dignity in one's manner.
- Winning legal cases.
- Getting the upper hand in situations.

GRAPHIEL – INTELLIGENCE OF MARS

Qualities of Graphiel are listed in Sloane 3821 as:
- To gain and overcome all warlike judgements and petitions.
- To overcome all manner of enemies and prevent them conquering.
- To compel enemies to submit.
- To stop the flow of blood from a wound.
- To fetch any person or cause them to come from anywhere in the world.
- To end all controversies and quarrels.
- To conquer powerful people and cause them to submit or be ruined.

Other qualities associated with Mars that could be considered are:
- Skill at acting.
- Courage in the face of adversity.
- Strength of mind giving resistance to fear and terror.

NACHIEL/NAKHIEL – INTELLIGENCE OF THE SUN

Qualities of Nachiel are listed in Sloane 3821 as:
- To gain renown, and be amiable and patient.
- To elevate a person to a position of power.
- To enable a person to do whatever they please.
- To cause a person to journey without delay or return without delay.
- To cause a person to contact you within thirty minutes.

Other qualities associated with the Sun that could be considered are:
- Development of the imagination.
- Ability to give good advice.
- Ability to distinguish right from wrong and act accordingly.
- Charity to others.

HAGIEL – INTELLIGENCE OF VENUS

Qualities of Hagiel are listed in Sloane 3821 as:
- To end conflict and strife.
- To gain agreement.
- To gain the love of another person.
- To help women with fertility issues.
- To dispel enchantments.
- To cause peace between a couple.
- To make animals fertile.
- To compel evil people to be good.

Other qualities associated with Venus that could be considered are:
- Development of personal beauty.
- Increase of desire.
- Sweetening of nature, could apply to self or others.
- Giving the power of hope.

TIRIEL – INTELLIGENCE OF MERCURY

Qualities of Tiriel are listed as:
- To make a person grateful for what they have and more affable.
- To get away with doing what you want.
- To have gains in wealth and prevent poverty.
- To gain greater understanding in divination.
- To gain eloquence and confidence when presenting.
- To gain quickness of understanding.
- To gain prudence in managing situations.
- To be temperate and thoughtful.
- To gain instructions or knowledge through dreams.

Other qualities associated with Mercury that could be considered are:
- Clarity of mind in difficult situations.
- Ability to act quickly when needed.

Malcha/Malcha Betarsisim[16] – Intelligence of the Moon

Qualities of Malcha are listed as:
- To make anyone friendly, pleasant and grateful to you.
- To remove malice and ill will directed at you from people (evil eye).
- To cause security by increasing your abundance.
- To increase riches and bodily health.
- To drive away enemies and evil beings from any place.

Other qualities associated with the Moon that could be considered are:
- Developing growth of plants and crops.
- Ability to cause something to increase or decrease.
- Ability to soothe troubles.
- Skill in giving good advice and direction.

---

[16] The longer name is given by Agrippa as the Intelligence of Intelligences of the Moon without explanation as to the difference to the other Intelligences. It is more commonly used as Malcha in later texts, as seen in the conjuration, and I have given the sigil for this accordingly.

TIMINGS

The conjuration of a Planetary Intelligence will obviously take place on its planetary day and during the planetary hour.[17] As the entire process is likely to take longer than the planetary hour, the activation of the magic circle and other actions prior to the conjuration will take a chunk of this time. It is worth rehearsing the practice previously to see how long the sequence takes to ensure the conjuration begins with the planetary hour. As long as this is the case, then the flow of the planetary energy has been established and it is not a problem if the conjurations or communication run into the next planetary hour. This can often occur, especially if the conjuration has to be repeated several times as is commonly the case.

Whilst the day and hour are the inflexible aspects that should not be altered, it is also worth considering what else is going on in the heavens. It is interesting to note from the grimoires that the planets were not all perceived as having positive relationships. A summary of the planetary relationships taken from the work of Agrippa is given in the following table.

Relationship	Sun	Mercury	Venus	Moon	Mars	Jupiter	Saturn
Sun towards		Enemy	Love	Enemy	Enemy	Love	Friend
Mercury towards	Enemy		Friend	Enemy	Enemy	Friend	Friend
Venus towards	Love	Love		Love	Love	Love	Enemy
Moon towards	Enemy	Enemy	Friend		Enemy	Friend	Friend
Mars towards	Enemy	Enemy	Love	Enemy		Enemy	Enemy
Jupiter towards	Friend	Friend	Friend	Friend	Enemy		Friend
Saturn towards	Friend	Friend	Enemy	Friend	Enemy	Friend	

---

17 How to calculate the planetary hours is included in Appendix I. There are also apps and websites that can do this now for the less mathematically minded.

It is easy to find online sites that cast the astrological chart for a given time, date, and location. Putting in your preferred option(s) will give you the information that shows if there are negative planetary aspects (enemy) which could have a detrimental effect on the planetary energy at the time of your conjuration. The aspects you most want to avoid are conjunctions, oppositions, and squares.[18] If it is possible to have none or as few as possible of these in the chart for you planned time, then this is the optimum.

This does not mean the conjuration will fail if there are any of these aspects. Minimising them adds to the magical momentum by removing 'friction' between the planets. At the end of the day all the other practices you have carried out will hopefully have ensured sufficient magical momentum for successful conjuration and communication, and this then becomes a minor consideration. However it is always good to maximise the magical momentum so this aspect is one that should be considered and planned for when choosing the conjuration timing if possible.

---

18 Oppositions and squares are considered challenging aspects, and conjunction is a combining of energies, which is not desired when it is an enemy relationship.

THE TOOLS AND THEIR CONSECRATIONS

CONSECRATION IS INCLUDED REPEATEDLY ACROSS MANY OF THE GRIMOIRES, and there is even an early grimoire dedicated to it.[19] The reasons for this emphasis on consecration are fourfold:

Bonding – the consecration creates a connection or bond between the user and the item, to the extent that with some items they may be seen as an extension of the person using them. For this reason the person using the item should be the one who consecrates it, e.g. conjuror consecrates the sword, skryer consecrates the crystal, etc.

Respect – by consecrating everything that is brought into the magic circle, you are showing respect for the spirits and deity/deities you work with. Respect is an essential component not just of spirit communication, but also how the magician engages with the worlds and all within them.

Purity of the sacred – consecration is part of the process of purifying oneself as well as one's tools for engaging in spirit/divine communication. As such it is a sacred act of preparation and purification which contributes to the mental and spiritual focus of the magician.

Magical Momentum – the energy and focus you put in to the consecrations adds to the magical momentum of your conjuration and increases the likelihood of success.

All the items present in the space where you perform the conjuration, whether indoors in a temple or outdoors in a secluded spot, should be consecrated. This list of items includes the sword, book, robe, holy oil, olive oil, holy water, crystal, burin, pestle and mortar, containers, censer/oil burner, incense/oils, glasses/contact lenses, any jewelry worn, including piercings, and circle if using a prepared circle that is transported to the site. If any chairs or cushions are used for comfort or practicality due to physical ailments, these should also be consecrated, as should a lectern if used.

Items that will not be used for a while prior to the conjuration should be stored in consecrated white silk in a dark space. Anything which you wear all the time like jewelry or piercing jewelry is best consecrated just prior to the conjuration. Unless otherwise stated consecrations are usually performed on your altar or table of practice. Over the years I have

---

19 *Liber Consecrationum* (*The Book of Consecrations*), c. 1400 CE.

become quite minimalist in my practices, so I only include items which are necessary and relevant in this work.[20]

I recommend consecrating the robes first, so you can wear them whilst performing the other consecrations, and the pen and silk cloths that other items will be wrapped in.[21] You may also wish to construct the magic circle first if you are going to have a permanent one, as doing all the work in the circle you are going to conjure in adds further to the magical momentum, increasing the likelihood of success.

Note that all consecrations should be performed in a magic circle, and on a waxing moon. The item will usually be placed on a small table or altar. This action also adds to the magical momentum of the rite. Unless otherwise stated, face east when performing consecrations. If a day is not stated for the consecration, Sunday is the default. This does not apply to perishable items like candles and incense, which should be consecrated on the appropriate planetary day and hour of the Intelligence who will be conjured. Whenever there is a ✠ in the text you recite, it indicates making the sign of the cross with your preferred hand.

Whilst it is not traditional grimoire practice, when reciting the words of the consecration I visualize a column of brilliant white light descending from the heavens and surrounding me and filling me. I then see this divine energy transmitted as golden light[22] from my heart down my arms to my hand(s) and from them into the item being consecrated. This is a practice I have added in over the years for efficacy and is entirely optional.

---

20 Writing about the *Heptameron*, Jim Baker observed 'The list of necessary equipment is also quite basic and lacks any obsessive requirements for its acquisition and consecration, a notable stumbling block (or excuse for failure) in later grimoires'. *Inquiry into Necromancy*, 2024. This agrees with my views on just using what is essential and not fetishizing the equipment to the extent of obsession.

21 If you wear glasses or contact lenses, consecrate these at the same time as the robes.

22 The transformation from white light to gold reflects the absorption of divine love and transmission of the same through you as the physical vessel of that love, coloured with the gold of the heart.

Book

The magical book acts as an incredibly useful repository of prayers (including Psalms), conjurations, spirit and divine names, seals and characters. The Pentacle of Solomon is usually drawn on the first page of the book.[23] The consecration of the book is unsurprisingly the most complex of all consecrations, taking place over the seven days of a week.

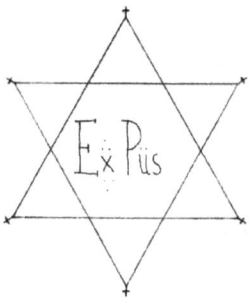

Consecration of the Book

This consecration is performed each day, in the appropriate planetary hour,[24] beginning on Saturday. Kneeling facing east in front of a small table covered with a white cloth, with the book open at the first page, and a lamp overhead,[25] recite this prayer and suffumigate the book with an appropriate planetary incense (for that day):

Adonay, Elohim, El, Eheieh Asher Eheieh, Prince of Princes, Existence of Existences, have mercy upon me, and cast Thine eyes upon Thy servant [N], who invoke Thee most devotedly, and supplicates Thee by Thy Holy and tremendous name Tetragrammaton to be propitious, and to order Thine Angels and Spirits to come and

---

23 As the book is consecrated, this provides the magician with an additional Pentacle of Solomon in the circle should it ever be needed. Also ensure the book is large with a lot of pages, as you are sure to add to it over time.

24 So this will be the first planetary hour after sunrise or the eighth. Preferably the first for the symbolism of the rise of the illuminating sun.

25 This is the one time where an overhead electric light is acceptable in conjuration. The light is left on for the entire seven days, day and night, which is safer than having a lit hanging lamp unattended for this time period. The curtains are kept closed for this entire period.

take up their abode in this place; O you Angels and Spirits of the Stars, O all you Angels and Elementary Spirits, O all you Spirits present before the Face of God, I the Minister and faithful Servant of the Most High conjure you, let God himself, the Existence of Existences, conjure you to come and be present in this Operation, I, the Servant of God, most humbly entreat you. Amen.[26]

After the prayer is said, leave the book on the table. This room should not be entered by anybody else or used for anything else during this week.

Burin

The burin[27] is a utility tool used for engraving and carving items. It usually has a white or horn handle.

Consecration of the Burin

It is consecrated in the hour and day of Jupiter (as is the needle if used for sewing, and for which the same consecration may be used). Recite over it:

I conjure thee, O instrument of steel, by God the Father Almighty, by the virtue of the heavens, of the stars, and of the angels who preside over them; by the virtue of stones, herbs, and animals; by the virtue of hail, snow, and wind; that thou receives such virtue that thou may obtain without deceit the end which I desire in all things wherein I shall use thee; through God the Creator of the Ages, and Emperor of the angels. Amen.

Then recite Psalms 3, 9, 31, 42, 60, 130.

Perfume with frankincense, sprinkle with exorcised water, and wrap it in silk saying:

Dani, Zumech, Agalmaturod, Gadiel, Pani, Caneloas, Merod, Gamidoi, Baldoi, Metatron, Angels most holy, be present as a guard for this instrument.

---

26 *Key of Solomon*. Skinner & Rankine, 2008:327, 361-362.
27 The old English name for the burin is a graver, due to its use in engraving.

Censer/Oil Burner

The use of fragrance in conjuration is vital, it is a significant part of the process of attracting the attention of the spirits.

Consecration of the Censer/Oil Burner

Anoint the censer/oil burner with holy oil, reciting:

You journeyed to the king with oil, and multiplied your perfumes; you sent your envoys far off, and sent down even to Sheol. You were wearied with the length of your way, but you did not say, 'It is hopeless'; you found new life for your strength, and so you were not faint.[28]

Crystal or Mirror

The crystal, glass ball, or mirror is used as a focus by the skryer for spirit contact, and as a portal for communication with the conjured spirit. Ideally the crystal or glass ball should be free of impurities or blemishes and at least four inches (ten centimetres) in diameter. Quartz is the most commonly used material for the crystal ball, but other crystals like obsidian or citrine quartz are also recorded so if it works for the skryer that is the key point. Magic mirrors are usually made of obsidian, and should not be a simple reflective mirror, as this can hinder the focus of the skryer. A number of grimoires use the phrase 'crystal or glass receptacle', so note that a glass ball is perfectly acceptable as an alternative to a crystal.[29] The skryer should test beforehand if they are comfortable skrying in a crystal placed on the floor, or if a small table or stand placed in the triangle is needed to raise the crystal off the ground for clearer vision of the crystal or mirror. If this is used it can be consecrated with the Consecration of Miscellaneous Items.

---

28 Again surprisingly there is no consecration of the censer in the grimoires. I created a simple consecration, using Isaiah 57:9-10.

29 Significantly, quartz and glass both have the same chemical formula, silicon dioxide.

Consecration of the Crystal

Sit in front of the crystal placed on a small table, and recite:

Oh, God! Who art the author of all good things, strengthen, I beseech thee, thy poor servant, that I may stand fast, without fear, through this dealing and work; enlighten, I beseech thee, oh Lord! the dark understanding of thy creature, so that my spiritual eye may be opened to see and know thy angelic spirits descending here in this crystal: (lay hand on the crystal,) and thou, oh inanimate creature of God, be sanctified and consecrated, and blessed to this purpose, that no evil fantasy may appear in thee; or, if they do gain ingress into this creature, they may be constrained to speak intelligibly, and truly, and without the least ambiguity, for Christ's sake. Amen. And forasmuch as thy servant here standing before thee, oh, Lord! desires neither evil treasures, nor injury to their neighbour, nor hurt to any living creature, grant them the power of skrying those celestial spirits or Intelligences, that may appear in this crystal, and whatever good gifts, whether the power of healing infirmities, or of imbibing wisdom, or discovering any evil likely to afflict any person or family, or any other good gift Thou may be pleased to bestow on me, enable me, by Thy wisdom and mercy, to use whatever I may receive to the honour of Thy Holy Name. Grant this for Thy son Christ's sake. Amen.[30]

Place the crystal in a white silk cloth or bag.

Pen

Whilst a goose feather and magical ink are traditional, a good quality ink pen is equally as valid.[31] Magic tends to use the technology available, so a nice ink pen or even rollerball pen if you have problems writing with a fountain pen is fine. This pen will be decorated and used only for magical work. Do not use something like a cheap biro, as this shows lack of effort and cheapens your work. You may wish to acquire either red ink cartridges to supplement the black, or buy a second pen if using a rollerball. (This consecration can also be used on a pencil for drawing the outline of the magic circle and the brushes for painting it).

---

30 Adapted with minor change from the consecration of the crystal in pseudo-Trithemius' *The Art of Drawing Spirits into Crystals*. If using a mirror replace the word crystal with mirror in the consecration.

31 The *Key of Solomon* also specifies a carved wooden box to store the feather in, possibly to protect it due to the fragility of feathers. As pens are more durable this is not necessary and a simple prepared silk will suffice.

Consecration of the Pen

Performed on a Wednesday during the hour of Mercury. The following words are spoken over the pen:

Abrahy, Habglas, Samay, Thie, Domal, Altheol, Caver, Adonay, drive all malignity from this pen[32] destined for great workings and give it the necessary virtue to write all things which concern the Art.[33]

Ring

Magic rings are common in the grimoires, especially protective ones. If you chose to make a ring into your magic ring, or have one created, it will obviously need consecration before use. A ring is not a required item for conjuring the Planetary Intelligences, but I have included it here for completion, for future practice further down the path.

Consecration of the Ring

The ring should be placed on a small table or altar.

O thou creature of God, ring I conjure thee, which was blessed and anointed of King Solomon with olive oil. So I bless thee and adjure thee to be blessed through Jesus Christ, the Son of the living God; that thou may have the virtue and power for that purpose that thou art ordained for. And as in the Ark of God in the Old Testament, the golden ring was born. So be thou to this servant of God, N, a token of knowledge unto this faithful servant of the true science of calling of spirits; that when thou art held up, I may have help of thee; that through thy virtue, I may subdue the power of all evil spirits and compel them to show and make me a true answer of all such things as I desire; and to show me the truth of all hidden things and the secrets of spirits, to make me perfect through Jesus Christ our Lord. I conjure thee thou creature of God. Thou ring, in whose figure of roundness are all things in the world contained and all figures and perfect knowledge of science in the form of thee be fixed. I conjure thee by all the names of all the orders of angels; and all the motions of the planets and spheres; and by that high name of God, Tetragrammaton, that thou may have such virtue and influence of grace of Jesus Christ; that unto what spirit or spirits soever thou be shown, that

---

32 Replace 'pen' with 'pencil' or 'brush' if consecrating these items.
33 *Key of Solomon.* See Skinner & Rankine, 2008: 351.

it may be brought to such fear and favour of the bearer of it; that through this blessed name, they may be made afraid and obey by and by the precept and will of this faithful servant of God, N, and so ever continue except if I licence them to depart; and that they have no power to lie, nor to tell any false tales, nor work guiles or falsehood where thou art shown; but that thou be unto this magician, through the Grace of God that works in thee, a blessed and consecrated ring, through the most blessed Son of God, who lives with God the Father and the Holy Spirit, world without end. Amen.[34]

Anoint with holy oil and then sprinkle with holy water. Then place on the appropriate finger.

Robe

By far the most common description of the robe in grimoires is one made of white linen. The robe should always be white unless there is a specific reason for it to be otherwise. Whilst there can be virtue in embroidering or marking the robe as mentioned in some grimoires, a simple white robe is generally perfectly fine. Although there are grimoires which give a whole range of clothing to wear together, a simple white robe and nothing underneath it is the norm.

Consecration of the Robe

The robe is wafted over burning frankincense whilst the conjuration is spoken:

Adonay, Agla, Eloy, Saday, Sabaoth, Tetragrammaton. And all you celestial Intelligences, guard me and preserve me from evil spirits, who could disturb the working which I am going to undertake with the aid of the Most High, whose holy name is Adonay, Adonay.[35]

---

34 Adapted from the consecration in *Liber Consecrationum*.

35 Surprisingly no grimoire gives a consecration of the robe, so I adapted the consecration of the silk for the purpose. *Key of Solomon.* Skinner & Rankine, 2008:356.

Silk Cloth

Silk cloth is traditionally used to wrap magical tools. It is generally regarded as being a good insulator of magical charge to preserve the consecration of the wrapped item. White is the usual colour for this silk, with black being used for items used with the dead. Items specific to a planet could be wrapped in a suitable planetary colour silk, but for all the general tools and items stick with white.

Consecration of the Silk Cloth

The day of consecration is not specified. Either Sunday or the same day as the first other consecrations are both fine. These characters are written on the silk.

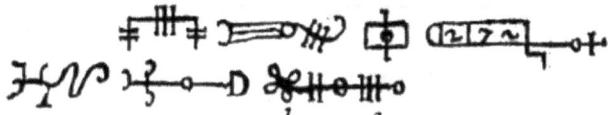

After this the silk is wafted over burning frankincense whilst the conjuration is spoken:

Adonay, Amosiath, Amarathon, Ensopen, Penmaton, Lamecheva, Catebsierop, Corbas. And all you celestial Intelligences, guard me and preserve me from evil spirits, who could disturb the working which I am going to undertake with the aid of the Most High, whose holy name is Adonay, Adonay.[36]

Sword

The sword is used to mark the magic circle when activating it, and as a symbol of authority, wielded to control spirits that may be troublesome.[37] Whilst some grimoires depict everyone bearing a sword, for practicality (especially indoors) it makes sense for only the conjuror to be bearing and wielding a sword. If the other practitioners feel the need for additional

---

36 *Key of Solomon*. Skinner & Rankine, 2008:356.

37 These may be other spirits attracted by the conjuration who decide to cause problems, not necessarily the ones you are conjuring.

protection, a black-handled knife will be equally efficacious, and is consecrated in the same manner as the sword.[38] The best known sword is the one shown in the *Key of Solomon*, which has these divine names engraved on it. The top line is on the blade and the second line on the cross-guard, and the name of Michael on the pommel.[39] If you are not familiar with wearing a sword in a scabbard, you may find it easier to have a simple frog (yes a holder is called this!) on a belt to have the sword hang by when not in use (both consecrated of course). This will make you very aware of wearing the sword and make you more careful and less likely to knock things over than a scabbard does. Alternatively, you can carry the sword into the circle, though having somewhere to place the sword for easy access can be useful. If the conjuror is also acting as the scribe, they may find it easier to place the sword on the floor whilst asking and recording questions.

יהוה : אדני : אהיה : ייאי :

אלהים : גבור :

Consecration of the Sword

In the day and hour of Jupiter, say:

---

38 For more details see the *Key of Solomon*.

39 From right to left Yahveh (IHVH) Adonay (ADNI) Eheieh (AHIH) Iiai (IIAI). Second row right to left on cross-guard Elohim Gibor (ALHIM GBVR) and pommel Michael (MIKAL). The name of the archangel Michael on the pommel indicates the sword as symbolic of the flaming sword of that archangel, and also gives a link between the sword and the triangle. Alternatively another version is to just have crosses around the names ✠ Agla ✠ On ✠ instead on the blade and nothing on the cross-guard.

I conjure thee, O sword, and I adjure and bind thee by the virtue of God the Father Omnipotent, by the virtue of Jesus Christ His Son, and by the Holy Spirit, and by all things made in heaven and earth, and by the perpetual virginity of Holy Mary, the blessed Mother of Our Lord, and by the chastity of John the Baptist, and by the dreadful day of doom, that thou be unto me a sword consecrated, that thou may be a bond and a help against all powers of Air, Water, Fire and Earth, such that whensoever this servant of God shall cast or show thee, all spirits may be made astonished until they are obedient unto me, and do whatsoever I command them. I conjure thee, sword, by the brightness and virtue of the flaming sword of the Kerubim, and by the sword of Solomon, and by Longinus' sword, that thou become blessed and consecrated, and that Our Lord Jesus Christ bless and dignify thee ✠ and sanctify thee ✠ that thou may overcome the gainsaying of all false spirits, by the virtue of Our Lord God Omnipotent Who shall come to judge the quick and the dead. World without end. Amen.[40]

Then anoint the pommel of the sword with holy oil and kiss the cross-guard.

Consecration of Materia Magica (Perishables)

Consecration of Candles (and Taper)

Whilst you may use matches or a lighter to light candles and charcoal, I personally prefer a simple white taper. This way you can use the same light for all of them. Recite these words over the candles (or taper):

I adjure thee effectively creature of fire in the names of the Supreme and Eternal God and by the ineffable name Yod Heh Vav Heh, and by the name Yah, and by the strongest name El, that the hearts of all spirits, whom we will call to this circle illuminated by you, that they may appear before us without all guile and fraud, through Him who created the body and lives forever and ever.[41]

---

40 The two-line consecration in the *Key of Solomon* feels wholly inadequate for such a significant item as the sword. For this reason I prefer to use an updated and amended version of the consecration given in *De Nigromancia*. MacDonald, 1987:34-35.

41 Translated from the Latin and adapted from *Experimentir Buch*. See Ortiz, 2018:43.

If you are using tea lights in oil burners, you can carve the seal of the Planetary Intelligence on the underneath of the tea lights with the burin or a consecrated needle (which is easier) before reciting the words.

Candles may be white, or the planetary colour, but should all be the same, and also unperfumed. Stick with the incense or oil for fragrance as that is what you have chosen and you will have previously tried it for smell before the conjuration.

Consecration of Incense

Recite these words over the incense:

God of Abraham, God of Isaac, God of Jacob, deign to bless these perfumes so that they may receive the strength and virtue necessary to attract good spirits, which I invoke in your Name.[42]

Consecration of Ink/Paint

Place the bottle of ink or cartridges on a small table or altar (or container of white paint or chalk), and say over them:

O Lord Jesus Christ, through your ineffable mercy spare me and pity me and hear me now, through the invocation of the name of the Trinity, of the Father, and of the Son, and of the Holy Spirit, in order that the prayers and words from my mouth are acceptable and pleasing to you, through the invocation of your one hundred holy names, namely Agla, Monhon and so on, humbly and faithfully begging you that you would sanctify and bless this ink by your most sacred names aforesaid, and by the name Shemhamphorash of seventy-two letters, that by the virtue, sanctity and power of the same names, and by your divine virtue and power, this same ink[43] *may be consecrated ✠ blessed ✠✠ strengthened ✠✠ through the virtue of your most holy body and blood that it may obtain the virtue and ability which it must possess, and effectually without any deceit, for correctly writing sacred seals, in order that it maintains the sacred virtue and has the power, for which it has been prepared, with the Lord providing, who sits in the highest place, to Whom be praise, honour and glory forever and ever. Amen.*[44]

---

42 *Key of Solomon*. See Skinner & Rankine, 2008: 346.

43 Replace 'ink' with 'chalk' or 'paint' here if consecrating them.

44 Adapted from the *Sworn Book of Honorius*. See Peterson, 2016:287-289.

Consecration of Oil

The oil may be consecrated once it is ready for use.

Oh Lord Jesus Christ the good shepherd, of thy omnipotent majesty & goodness, vouchsafe to cast thy holy Eyes upon this Oil, & to ✠ *consecrate* ✠ *bless &* ✠ *sanctify this Oil by the virtue of thy holy name & Jehovah* ✠ *Tetragrammaton* ✠ *Agla* ✠ *Sabaoth, Saday* ✠ *Adonay* ✠ *Eloy* ✠ *& by the virtue of the blessed Virgin Mary thy mother, & which of thine humility did leave thy father's seat in heaven, & did dwell with thy mother as an Infant, vouchsafe I beseech thee to bless this Oil that I may see & bind these spirits which you have created, & that I may speak with them whenever I will, through Jesus Christ our Lord Amen.*[45]

Consecration of Paper/Parchment

Speak the words over the sheets of paper or parchment:

I conjure Thee, King of Angels, El Saday ✠ *that this paper (/parchment) be of use to me upon which I may write all things regarding the Magical Arts or Workings which I will perform in Thy Holy Name.*[46]

Consecration of Holy Water

The water used should be 'living water', i.e. water gathered from a spring, stream or river (it should also not have been drawn from a conduit by human hand). This should preferably be gathered at sunrise. A glass or ceramic vessel is recommended to hold this water. As you gather the water say:

God, who art the truth and the life, deign to sanctify this water, which I need to use in my workings.[47]

---

[45] *Boxgrove Manual.* See Klaasen 2019:113. Note this consecration can be used for both the Holy Oil and Olive Oil.
[46] Adapted from the *Key of Solomon.* See Skinner & Rankine, 2008:354.
[47] See *Key of Solomon.* Skinner & Rankine, 2008:347.

Add salt and recite Psalms 102, 54, 6.[48]

Note whilst the aspergillum made of collected herbs is often mentioned for use asperging the holy water, a spring of hyssop works fine, and also fits nicely with the blessing "Purge me with hyssop ....".[49]

Consecration of Miscellaneous Other Items

Consecration of Charcoal Blocks

I exorcise you charcoal through Him Who created all things, that every fantasy or phantasm leaves you immediately so that they do not harm us. O Lord, almighty God, bless this charcoal that will burn for the praise and honour of Your Name, so that no harm can befall us, through our Lord Jesus Christ, who lives and reign for ever and ever, Amen.[50]

Consecration of Glasses/Contact Lenses

Oh, God! Who art the author of all good things, strengthen, I beseech thee, thy servant, that I may stand fast, without fear, through this dealing and work; enlighten, I beseech thee, oh Lord! my dark understanding, so that my spiritual eye may be opened to see and know thy spirits through this object of clear vision: (place preferred hand on glasses or tray of lenses) *and thou, oh object of clear vision, be sanctified and consecrated, and blessed to this purpose, that no evil fantasy may appear in thee truly, and without the least ambiguity, for Christ's sake.* ✠ (Make cross over glasses/lenses with preferred hand) Amen.[51]

Consecration of Jewelry

O thou creature of God, thou [item] I conjure thee, I bless thee and adjure thee to be blessed through Jesus Christ, the Son of the living God; that thou may have the virtue

---

48 Recite the Psalms in Latin, English or your native language, whichever you feel most comfortable with.

49 As previously stated I prefer to only use necessary paraphernalia and save the aspergillum for workings from the *Key of Solomon*, etc.

50 Adapted from consecration of the fire in *Experimentir Buch*. See Ortiz, 2019:45

51 Adapted from the consecration of the crystal in pseudo-Trithemius' *The Art of Drawing Spirits into Crystals*.

and power for that purpose that thou art ordained for, through the most blessed Son of God, who lives with God the Father and the Holy Spirit, world without end. Amen.

Anoint with olive oil and then sprinkle with holy water.[52]

Miscellany

This consecration can be used on any other items which require consecration but do not have their own specific consecration, e.g. pestle and mortar, storage jars and bottles, candlesticks, chair or cushion, safety pins for attaching lamen to chest of robe, etc. You can use this for matches and lighter, or if you prefer you can use the consecration for candles.

Consecration of Miscellaneous Items[53]

I bless you [item] by God the Father ✠ the Son ✠ and the Holy Ghost ✠, with the highest and undivided Trinity, and with the Creator of these creatures, that you be useful for this project. I bless you also with all the angels and Holy God in Heaven ✠ and by the Mightiest Names: Tetragrammaton, Agla, Hagios, Atheos, Athanatos, Yehyros, Eleyson, Vnies; by the four elements, by the Firmament of Heaven, and by all the Holy Words which were previously spoken. Amen.

---

52 This is a greatly shortened version of the ring consecration from *Liber Consecrationum*. Note I replaced the holy oil with olive oil as items like piercings may be through areas which would be sensitive to the contents of the holy oil.

53 Abbreviated version of the 'Blessing for All Things' from *Experimentir Buch*. Ortiz, 2018:45.

FRAGRANCES

THE USE OF INCENSE IS ANCIENT, GOING BACK TO PRE-HISTORY. AT SOME point the connection between pleasant fragrances which left an intangible presence, and spirits, who can also be perceived as intangible presences, was made. From here the connection of offering fragrances to attract the attention of spirits, to make requests of them or placate them, was a logical development.

Whilst it would be a nice connection to use the planetary incenses given in Agrippa's *Three Books of Occult Philosophy*, where the Intelligences are first mentioned, this is not practical. These recipes include animal parts and minerals and inhaling them is not very conducive to good health. Using a single resin rather than a blended incense has the beneficial effect of not smelling like a bonfire after a while, and not requiring a lot of time blending it. I have nothing against blending incenses and have done so personally for over forty years, but for conjuring the Intelligences pure resin works very well.

A practical alternative to incense which may be preferable circumstances is to use oil burners instead. For this you use appropriate essential oils, or blends of essential oils diluted in holy water and released via the burners during the ceremony. The key factor in suffumigation is that the fragrances are pleasing to the spirits, and so using oil burners to release the fragrance achieves the same result without clouds of smoke, or the deterioration in quality of fragrance that occurs as the burning incense reaches the plant material smell. The absence of smoke can be helpful if you are indoors (remember smoke detectors need disabling if you are burning incense), especially if any of the practitioners suffer from asthma or other bronchial or breathing issues which could be triggered by copious amounts of smoke. Another benefit of oil burners is that unlike censers they do not need to be topped up as they will release fragrance for a long period of time.

The seal of the Planetary Intelligence can also be carved into the tea lights/candles so that it is released with the fragrance emphasising the connection to the spirit and its seal. With these sorts of candles, the temperature is not so high that the release of the seal as the candle burns will be painful to it like the burning of the seal in coercion.

Planet	Resin	Oil
Sun	Frankincense	Orange or Cinnamon
Mercury	Mastic	Lemon or Rosemary
Venus	Amber	Rose or Sandalwood
Moon	Galbanum	Jasmine or Camphor
Mars	Opoponax	Aloe or Ginger
Jupiter	Benzoin	Cedar or Juniper
Saturn	Myrrh	Pine or Patchouli

Making Holy Oil

The Holy Oil[54] frequently mentioned in the grimoires and used for anointing is that given in the Bible, in Exodus 30:22-25. It is made with two parts each of cassia bark and myrrh resin, and one part each of calamus root and cinnamon, which after being ground as fine as possible are added to olive oil. The quantity of olive oil is one quarter of the combined weight of the four ingredients, so if the parts were ounces, giving six ounces total, you would use one and a half ounces of olive oil as the base to add the four ingredients to. This is then left to mature in a glass container in a cool dark place, for at least a lunar month, and strained afterwards for the oil, leaving the solids behind.

Alternatively you can make a quick version using the essential oils for each of the ingredients; however, if you do this the quantity of olive oil needs to be increased or the resulting oil may be somewhat caustic to sensitive skin. In this case go with something like twenty drops each of cassia and myrrh oils, ten drops each of calamus and cinnamon, and one hundred and eighty drops of virgin olive oil. Calamus oil can be very difficult to get.

This is not a recipe where any of the items should be substituted, as it is the standard anointing oil of the grimoire tradition, which was also given as the oil in *Abramelin*.

---

54 In some grimoires you will see consecrated holy oil referred to as chrism.

THE LEAD-IN

THE FIRST TIME YOU PERFORM A CONJURATION IT IS ADVISABLE TO SPEND seven days on the preparation prior to the actual ceremony. The actual conjuration takes place on the eighth day, and the first day is a preparation of items day, with the purificatory process beginning on the second day and lasting for a week. Once you have performed a successful conjuration this can be reduced to a preparatory day the previous week (on the same day of the week as the conjuration), a three day break and then subsequently three days of purification and the conjuration on the fourth day.

The sequence of preparation involves fasting, prayer, and purificatory baths, with a confession on the day of the conjuration prior to the commencement of the planetary hour. It is also a good idea to say the conjuration each day, rehearsing it so that when you perform the conjuration you have familiarity and do not stumble over it at all.

As a bare minimum, you should have the day of the conjuration and the following day off work. If it is possible having as much of the fasting period off work as possible too is a good idea.

Fasting

Fasting, or abstinence, is mentioned in a number of grimoires as part of the preparation to conjuration. Before fasting I would strongly encourage checking with a medical professional before starting it (a doctor, not a friend who thinks they know it all), especially if you have any pre-existing medical conditions.

I would strongly discourage seven days of only water. If you have ever done this, you will know that by the end of the week your mind is wandering and your body is confused. This is not a state to be performing conjuration in, and should be avoided. However starting some of the abstinence at seven days is a good idea. At the seven-day period, begin the abstinence from alcohol, caffeine, drugs (except those prescribed by your doctor), fish, meat, nicotine, swearing, and sexual activity (including masturbation), so that at the one-day mark, the full fast may begin.[55] For the last day you should only drink water and eat nothing. If this is going to be a struggle or you find yourself starting to get a little mentally fuzzy, drink pure apple juice[56] to keep your blood sugar up. Personally, I recommend including the apple juice; it has always worked well for me.

There is a second type of fast to include which is a product of the modern world: the electronic fast. As the physical fast works to purify the body, so the electronic fast works to purify the mind. For the seven days prior to the conjuration, avoid social media, gaming, and television as much as possible. Ideally this should be a complete abstinence, though if you need to check emails this is fine. Certainly avoid gaming, watching television, regularly checking your mobile, or binging on Netflix, and indulging in social media like Facebook, Instagram, Tik-Tok, etc.

Remember that fasting is a purificatory process, and you should commit fully to it as part of the process of building magical momentum. Another abstinence which is mentioned in the grimoires as part of this process is abstinence from swearing. Swearing and cursing can be seen as profaning the mouth which you will be using to utter sacred names. Avoid swearing, and consider gargling each day with holy water as part of your purification to prepare your mouth for the conjuration. In *Experimentir-Buch* the practice of placing a small piece of frankincense resin in the mouth before conjuration is mentioned. This may have been to act as a purification of the words being spoken.

It is also a good idea to minimize (or even cut out) socialization during this period, as you are more likely to let your guard down with friends, and allow your focus to be dispersed, as well as increase the chance of swearing.

Purificatory Baths

Run the bath (not too hot or too cold). Take a small quantity of rock salt (5ml) and bless it saying:

---

55 Note for future reference, if you are doing a major angelic or demonic conjuration, the last three days on just water and apple juice is recommended if possible, with eating an apple if needed at any point. Also note that this final period of the fast is a complete fast and not a daylight fast where food is eaten during the hours of darkness.

56 Or a different natural pure juice if you cannot drink apple.

I bless thee in the name of the Father, the Son and the Holy Ghost. Amen. The blessing of God the Almighty Father be upon thee and all goodness enter into thee wherefore I bless thee and sanctify thee that thou help me.

Add the salt to the bath saying:

Benediciti omnia opera Domino ✠.[57]

Now add x[58] drops of the appropriate planetary essential oil to the bath. The planetary oil added each day is that of the Planetary Intelligence conjured (i.e., it is not the oil of the planet of the day), adding to the magical momentum and focus of the practitioner.

The Penitential Psalms[59] are recited whilst in the bath so it becomes a purification of body, mind, and spirit.[60]

After washing get out of the bath and dry yourself with a clean white towel (clean each day). Do not use a hairdryer to dry your hair, as this could have a distracting or dispersing effect on you after the focus you have achieved whilst bathing.

On the day of the conjuration, you will have your robe ready to put on after bathing. Sprinkle yourself with blessed water and say:

Purge me, O Lord, with hyssop, and I shall be clean; wash me, and I shall be whiter than snow, for to Thee is all power, Who has always been and will be until all Eternity. In Thee is my confidence and I cannot stray under Thy direction.[61]

---

57 'Blessed are all the works of the Lord'. Note the crosses being made in the bathing are not traditional, I added them out of preference. Use or discard as you prefer.

58 Where x is the number of the planet of the Intelligence, so 3 if it is Saturnian, 4 is Jupiterian, 5 if Martial, 6 if Solar, 7 if Venusian, 8 if Mercurial or 9 if Lunar.

59 The Penitential Psalms were collated by Cassiodorus in the 6th Century CE and are chanted every day during Lent. They are Psalms 6, 31, 37, 50, 101, 129, and 142. Dee used them as part of the preparation for his work, and they are often used in the period prior to conjuration in the same way. Whilst I prefer to recite the Psalms in Latin, English or another language if it is your native tongue are equally fine.

60 See *Key of Solomon*. Skinner & Rankine, 2008:341. Same for the recitation whilst robing on the day of conjuration.

61 Psalm 51:7.

After drying and as you dress say these words:

Ancor, Amade, Theodanea, Paneor, Amitor. By the merit of the Holy Angels, I will clothe and dress myself, Lord [begin to dress at this point], *with the garments of salvation and may you permit me to come to the end of the things which I wish for and by your help, I will succeed in finishing this Work. Grant me, Most Holy Adonay* ✠ *the kingdom which reigns for all the Ages. Amen.*

Confession

The confession is mentioned in a number of grimoires, and can cause a knee-jerk reaction in some people. The confession is said by yourself on the day of the conjuration, and does serve important functions. The confession acts as a reminder to avoid ego inflation, and also to clear the mind of distractions. After bathing on the day of the conjuration is a good time to perform the confession, so you go into the conjuration in humility with a pure mind and pure body. Beyond the rite, it is also a reminder of the importance of compassion, which is one of the most powerful virtues the practitioner possesses.

The confession given in the *Key of Solomon* is long and I do not use it or include it as I feel a lot of the content will not apply to most people and may have a jarring effect detrimental to the focus you should have going into the conjuration. You the practitioner know what you need to be saying in your confession. However the prayer to be said after the confession in the *Key of Solomon* can be recited usefully:

Lord God, all powerful, eternal and Father of all creatures, pour out on me and let me feel the effects of Thy mercy and graciousness, as much as I am Thy creature, defend me from my enemies, and confirm in me a steadfast and secure devotion, Oh Lord, I commend my body and soul to Thee and I place my hope only in Thee. I found it on Thee alone, oh Lord my God, aid me and grant my wishes on that day or hour when I may invoke Thee, be Thou my succour and give me a new heart according to Your mercy, these are the gifts which I await from Thee, oh my Master and my God who lives and reigns unto the Ages of the Ages. So mote it be.[62]

---

62 See *Key of Solomon*. Skinner & Rankine, 2008:291.

Summary of Preparation

Day -7	Check long-range weather forecast for day of conjuration if working outdoors[63]
	Prepare seal and lamens, oil, incense for the conjuration
Day -6	Begin fast, purificatory bath with Psalms
Day -5 to Day -2	Purificatory bath with Psalms
Day -1	Full fast, purificatory bath with Psalms
Day of Conjuration	Purificatory bath with Psalms, put on robe
	Confession
	Preparation of space
	Conjuration sequence

List of Items for the Conjuration

This is a checklist of all the essential items (consecrated) you should have prepared and ready for the conjuration:

- Magic Circle
- Triangle
- Sword
- Robes
- Seal for under crystal in triangle
- Lamens for practitioners (with safety pins to attach to the chests of the robes)
- Book of Conjurations
- Crystal with stand or Magic Mirror
- Lighter or Matches (plus Taper if you use)
- 3 Candles and Candlesticks for the triangle (white or planetary colour)

---

[63] Whilst these are not always 100% accurate, they should at least give an indication of severe weather conditions which could prevent the conjuration.

- 4 Candles and Candlesticks for the Circle[64] (white or planetary colour)
- Censer with charcoal blocks and resin, or Oil Burner with tea light and essential oil (holy water can be used to dilute the oil)
- Container of Holy Water
- Container of Holy Oil
- Container of Olive Oil
- Pen and Ink
- Spare Pages of Paper (at least two with the planetary kamea on in case required for working out name sigils)
- List of questions to ask
- Any glasses/contact lenses/jewelry the practitioners are wearing

---

64 If possible tall candlesticks are good for this as they are more visible and less likely to be accidentally kicked over.

LICENSE TO REMAIN (OPTIONAL)

Many people who practice grimoire magic are also practitioners of other systems of magic. As a result they may have personal spirits and/or house spirits which they do not wish to push out of the home when performing a banishing. Additionally if the conjuration is outdoors in nature, the same principle applies of not being rude to the spirits whose home you may be intruding upon. If working outdoors the License to Remain is compulsory rather than optional, there is no point in risking upsetting local spirits who may then choose to interfere with your work. Additionally if you do have an outdoor spot in mind, check it out first and develop a relationship with any spirits of the area before just turning up to do a conjuration.[65] This may not have been the way in the past, but now we know better!

For this reason I created the License to Remain, which once created seemed ridiculously obvious as a practice to include. When performing a banishing (such as the Lesser Banishing Ritual of the Pentagram), perform the License to Remain first. The License uses the same divine names as the magic circle given in this conjuration (and in the LBRP). If you use a different form of banishing the divine names could be adjusted accordingly; the principle is the key thing here.

---

65 E.g. remove any rubbish you see in the area, make offerings which the spirits of the place indicate they would like such as milk, honey, wine, apples, tobacco, etc.

The License

Stand facing east, legs together, right arm raised with palm to the heavens, left arm by side with palm facing the ground

To all creatures who by right or invitation do dwell here, I give you license to remain, in the divine names:
Yahveh

Face south

Adonai

Face west

Eheieh

Face north

AGLA

Face east

Remain I say, remain, while all uninvited creatures and influences are banished.

ARARITA

THE TRIANGLE

THE TRIANGLE IS USED AS THE CONSTRAINING LOCUS, WITHIN WHICH THE crystal or mirror is placed. It may also contain talismans for consecration (see Appendix IV). For this operation the triangle from the *Goetia* is used, which is one of the most popular and oft used triangles. This triangle has the three divine names Primeumaton[66], Anaphexeton,[67] and Tetragrammaton around the edge, and Michael, the first amongst the archangels and considered to be the strongest around the circle in the centre where the crystal or mirror is placed.

CONSTRUCTION OF THE TRIANGLE

As this triangle is likely to be used repeatedly over the years, it is worth making a permanent one. A piece of white cloth or plain tan or light brown linoleum can be used as the base. Linoleum has the benefit of paint not spreading as it can on cloth. I would recommend eighteen to twenty-four inches (forty-five to sixty centimetres) as the side size, depending on

---

66 Primeumaton (Gk) – First Breath – the Creator, the name which is said to command the whole host of heaven.

67 Peterson argues convincingly that this is from Anekphoniton (Gk) – Unpronounceable, referring to the Tetragrammaton. As the Tetragrammaton is also known as the Unpronounceable Name, in this context we could read the triangle as saying 'The unpronounceable first breath of the Unpronounceable Name'. This implies the divine as the first cause which is ideal for the nature and role of the triangle as a locus of inter-realm communication, representing the place of first manifestation.

preference and considerations like space. You will see bigger triangles mentioned or advertised, but it is not necessary. The design is then painted on in black.[68]

LOCATION OF THE TRIANGLE

The triangle is placed outside the circle, with its base facing the circle. Some texts suggest a distance of two feet (sixty centimeters)[69] from the circle, however I recommend reducing this distance to one foot (thirty centimeters) as the distance from the circle edge to the crystal/mirror in the triangle should not be too great as to interfere with the skryer's vision of the crystal/mirror.

The triangle is placed according to the nature of the Planetary Intelligence, i.e. which planet it acts under the auspices of. For this a quick diversion into elemental theory is necessary. The attributions usually found in modern magical texts are recent, with a switch made by Eliphas Levi in the nineteenth century which ignored the many centuries of attribution since ancient Greece.[70] The Golden Dawn and all who followed used Levi's attributions without questioning or challenging them.

Levi switched the traditional fire being in the east (place of the rising sun, or big ball of fire) with air in the south. Water in the west and earth in the north were traditional attributions. This switch by Levi ignores the doctrine of elemental qualities. Each element has two qualities from the axis of cold-warmth and dry-moist. Thus each element shares one of its two qualities with the element on either side of it on the axis. So fire being dry and warm shares dryness with earth and warmth with air. The process of elemental interaction and transformation is all based on this axis, which Levi ignored. Therefore the triangle attributions given here use the traditional and logical attributions rather than the modern and flawed attributions.

---

68 There are a lot of variations of this, with different colour combinations and the use of black, white, and red letters. I am giving a simple option. Whenever possible keep it simple.

69 E.g., Sloane 2731, 'The triangle that Salomon Commanded the Disobedient Spirits Into; it is to be Made 2 foot off from the Circle'.

70 First discussed by Empedocles in the fifth century BCE in *Tetrasomia* (*Doctrine of the Four Elements*), and set into the standard directional format discussed by Zosimos of Panopolis in the late third-fourth century CE in his work *Upon the Letter Omega*. For more on this see my book *Practical Elemental Magick* 2008:36-42.

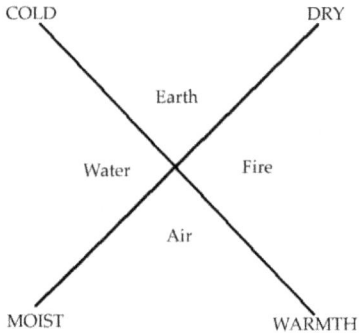

So applying the qualities of the planets, the direction for the Planetary Intelligences (and hence the triangle) are:

Planet	**Element**	**Direction**
Sun	Fire	East
Mars	Fire	East
Mercury	Air	South
Jupiter	Air/Water[71]	South-West
Moon	Water	West
Saturn	Earth	North
Venus	Earth	North

You will note that the positions of the elements in relation to each other are determined by their shared qualities. However, the directional attributions are a symbolic model to assist with codifying and rationalizing the forces of the universe for magical working. As the elements clearly do not just exist in one direction, the directions are based around the one universal visual absolute we have, that of the sun rising in the east. Thus, the fire of the rising sun forms the basis for the directional attributions.

If you are conjuring outdoors, there may be occasions where you rearrange the directional attributions of the elements. If you are working,

---

71 Agrippa attributes Jupiter to Air, but it was also seen as being watery due to its rulership of the water sign Pisces. Interestingly from a scientific point of view Jupiter is a gas giant (air) with a hue sea (water) of hydrogen.

for example, with a large body of water like an ocean or lake to the north of you, you might feel it is inappropriate for water to be symbolically in the west when it is so physically tangible in the north. The obvious solution is to move each elemental attribution clockwise until water is symbolically and physically in the same direction. This works for most occasions, unless you also have a large body of earth like mountains or wooded hills as well as a large body of water, and the earth is not in a direction 90° clockwise from the body of water. In such an instance the water and earth are assigned to the direction of their respective bodies. Fire is then attributed (east, south, or west are all fine as representing the daily journey of the sun) and air, which is all around us, is attributed to the last direction. Although this may not match to the symbolic model, at times the manifest physical takes precedence over the symbolic, preventing any mental dissonance.

If you do rearrange the elemental directions outdoors, remember to place your triangle accordingly based on the element of the planet. Note in this instance you can chose whether to put the Jupiter triangle in the direction attributed to water or air if they are not next to each other in the circle.

THE MAGIC CIRCLE

NONE OF THE GRIMOIRES GIVE A MAGIC CIRCLE ASSOCIATED WITH THE Planetary Intelligences, so I constructed a simple one. It is a single band circle, with the diameter of the outer and inner circles being ten and nine feet respectively (three hundred centimeters or three meters, and two hundred and seventy centimeters). I and a lot of other people have used this for this purpose successfully over the years.

The first consideration is whether this is going to be a temporary or permanent circle. If it is a temporary indoor circle, you should preferably draw it with blessed chalk.[72] You also need to consider if this is a circle you are able to leave up for a period of a week, or if you will need to rather construct it for the conjuration itself. If this is the case you will need to factor this in to the time before the planetary hour starts on the day of conjuration, as it takes longer than you think to draw a magic circle with chalk. This is something that is worth practicing to get an idea of the timescale, and also develop your skills at magic circle drawing. Having a central pole with a string measured to the length of the circle radius to

---

72 Some grimoires also use charcoal, but the white is preferable with the activation visualisation.

hold a pencil[73] for marking the circles is worth practicing until you can do it easily and make perfect circles. The chalk can then be drawn over the pencil markings around the circle clockwise, east to east. Drawing the divine names and pentagrams with chalk is also worth practicing. If you create a temporary circle outdoors, remember the ground needs to be flat and even, and allow extra time due to the differences you will experience.

A permanent circle has the benefit of being used again and again over the years. You need to acquire a piece of ten foot (three meter) square plain linoleum to cut into the circle. Cloth is an option, but can rumple and catch underfoot when moving in the circle and also take damage more easily. It does have the benefit of being storable in a smaller space however. This time you will be using white paint[74] to mark the circle and also the divine names and pentagrams. If you decide to write the names in Hebrew rather than English, it is worth practicing painting them first with the brush you are going to use, so you are confident and comfortable when you do them on your circle. Depending on the type of paint you use, you may wish to have a suitable solvent nearby so you can correct any mistakes when the paint has dried. Remember at this stage it is not being activated for use, so you can make corrections!

If you are making a linoleum-base circle for outdoor use, you may wish to consider getting an eleven foot square (three hundred and thirty centimeter) piece. In this instance you should not cut the circle out but paint it on so there is a border of six inches (fifteen centimeters) at the outer circle in the middle of the sides of the square. Then cut the square into four small equal squares, and in the space at the edge between the outside of the outer circle and the edge of the linoleum, add in a metal eyelet on each side (see illustration on page 44). The four squares are then connected and tied together to make the full-size circle at the site when you arrive. This practice of making portable outdoor circles to be constructed in this manner is actually described in grimoires.

---

73 And of course the pencil, string, and pole will be consecrated for use. The pencil can be consecrated as the pen, and the string and pole with the miscellaneous consecration. Remember the string is going to need to be longer than five feet to allow for tying around the rod and the pencil. Also a tape measure to ensure you have the right length is recommended, also miscellaneous consecration.

74 Again use the miscellaneous conjuration for paint, and the pen consecration for brushes.

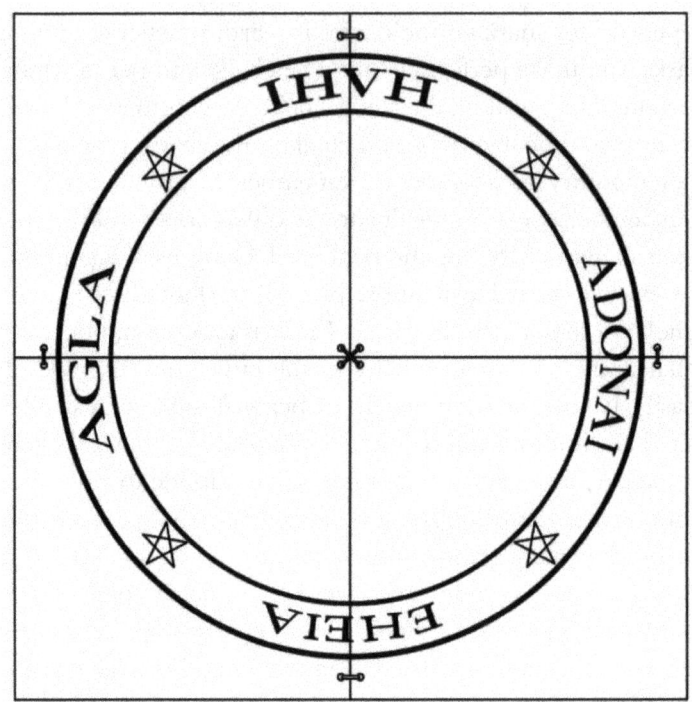

Outdoor Magic Circle

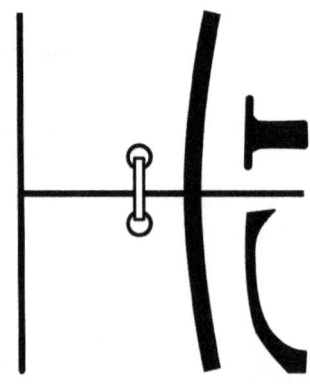

Close-up of Loops

The Conjuration Sequence

The sequence of a conjuration follows a number of steps. All the practitioners will already have bathed, prayed, performed the confession and prepared themselves and have all the required items to hand. Any phones in the house should be unplugged at the socket, and all mobiles switched off. Ideally turn off your television and internet router too. In fact unplug everything that is not essential to be plugged in. Disconnect the doorbell and smoke alarms temporarily for the duration of the ritual. This is for the dual purpose of avoiding disturbance and also because it is not unknown for electrical phenomena to occur during conjurations, so it is better to minimize the ability for this to occur.

The room or space should have the magic circle and triangle set up, with the crystal/mirror in place inside the triangle, and candles at the three corners of the triangle. If candles are being used for light, they should have already been placed inside the circle equidistant just a few centimeters inside the inner circle (e.g., four at the four directions).

The sequence then proceeds...

Activate the Crystal and Triangle

The skryer anoints the crystal with blessed olive oil, so there is a thin film of oil over the crystal. The conjuror places the seal of the Intelligence under the base the crystal is on (or base of the mirror), along with any talismans that may require charging.[75]

The conjuror activates the triangle first. With the tip of the sword, beginning at the apex of the triangle and proceeding clockwise, they trace the triangle, visualizing a burning white fire moving from the tip of the sword to the triangle. Any other practitioners present should also be visualizing during this procedure. The names around the triangle are then traced. However the names are traced anticlockwise (as they are for constraining rather than protecting), in the sequence Anaphexeton – Primeumaton – Tetragrammaton. As each name is traced the conjuror should intone the name. Finally the name of Michael is traced and intoned. This is done clockwise, as it is written, and because Michael is being acknowledged as the ruler of angels in a protective role.

---

75 See Appendix IV on Consecrating Talismans.

ENTER THE CIRCLE, ACTIVATE AND PREPARE IT

The conjuror followed by the skryer, scribe, and any others (if present) enter the circle from the north-east.[76] When all the practitioners are inside the magic circle, the conjurer marks the circumference of each band of the magic circle clockwise with the tip of the sword, seeing it burning with a white fire (the other practitioners should also be concentrating on this). This is done clockwise from East to East. Then the names in the band of the magic circle should be traced with the tip of the sword and intoned as this is done, and the pentagrams should also be traced.

When this is complete, the conjuror draws two circles in the air above the outer band of the circle, as high in the air as they comfortably can, again from East to East, saying:

I put the Seal of Solomon over us [/me] for salvation and defence, in order that it protects us [/me] in the face of the enemy. In the name of the Father and the Son and the Holy Spirit. Amen.[77]

The conjuror fumigates the circle from East to East, reciting the Incense Prayer:[78]

Have mercy on me O God according to Thy loving kindness, according to the multitude of Thy tender mercies. Blot out my transgressions, cleanse me from my sin, and bless both me, and these thy creatures of kinds, and increase Thy virtue, force and might in these odours, that no enemy nor vain visions, nor false delusions enter into them, but through Thy virtue, truth, and might, make them helpful to unto me/us through ✠ Jesus Christ ✠ our Lord, so be it done, Amen, fiat, Amen.

Note the same is done using an oil burner rather than censer if you have chosen this option.

---

76 This is the direction I was taught. No explanation was given, though I speculate it is because it is between the solidity of the earth in the north and the illuminating rays of the sun (rise) in the east.

77 See the *Sworn Book of Honorius*. Peterson, 2016:243. This serves the function of giving a more three dimensional feel to the magic circle, extending it from a two-dimensional circle to a three-dimensional cylinder

78 Adapted from prayer in *The Secret of Secrets*; a couple of minor word changes are the only adjustments made.

The conjuror then asperges the circle in the same manner (East to East) with blessed holy water, saying:

Out of his heart will flow rivers of living water.[79]

After this the conjuror lights any candles in the circle, starting in the East and moving clockwise round the circle (done after asperging to ensure no candles are put out by the water).

Prepare the participants

The conjuror should anoint themselves and any other practitioners with consecrated holy oil, saying each time:

You have been anointed by the Holy One, and you all have knowledge.[80]

The conjuror (standing in the centre of the circle) performs the blessing of the skryer, who kneels before the conjuror (the seer is kneeling so that their back is to the direction the triangle is in):[81]

I conjure you, skryer
By the Father ✠ *and Son* ✠ *and Holy Spirit* ✠*, to whose name all knees are bent and all voices proclaim Hosanna,* [Anoint eyes of seer[82] with olive oil[83]]
I conjure you, by the holy Mary ✠ *always virgin,*

---

79 John 7:38.

80 1 John 2:20.

81 Taken from a divination in the *Munich Handbook of Necromancy*, with a minor adaption replacing boy with skryer. The translation from the Latin and adaptation of the flow are my own. I have omitted a phrase at the end as it pertained to discovering a murder and is not appropriate here. The anointing of the eyes with holy anointing oil as an aid to spirit vision is given in *De Nigromancia*. Although called a conjuration, this is more of a blessing.

82 It is hugely important that only a tiny quantity of the olive oil be anointed **on the eyelids**; any oil in the eyes may result in extreme pain and the need to stop the whole conjuration. For a graphically amusing example of this see Lon Milo DuQuette's delightfully engaging autobiography *My Life with the Spirits* (1999). I suggest anointing the shape of the cross on the eyelids.

83 Olive oil is used to reduce risk of eye pain, but more significantly, because it establishes a sympathetic link with the crystal or mirror which has been anointed with the same consecrated olive oil.

By the angels ✠ and archangels ✠, by the four seniors ✠,
And by the thousands of martyrs who stumbled in the name of Christ ✠,
And by holy John the Baptist ✠, and by all the patriarchs ✠ and prophets ✠,
And by the twelve apostles ✠, and by the four evangelists ✠,
And by the seventy disciples ✠, and by all the saints who are holy men ✠ and holy women ✠,
And by all the powers of almighty God ✠, celestial, terrestrial, and infernal, so that whatever you see, you see truly through the power and grace of almighty God ✠.

The skryer then turns round to face the crystal and makes themselves comfortable for the communication.

Perform Preparatory Prayers

The conjuror, still standing in the centre of the circle, raises their eyes to heaven and recites a prayer to God:

O Lord, Holy Father and All-powerful, merciful God who has created all things, who knows and can do all things, to Whom nothing is hidden nor impossible and who is not ignorant of the fact that we do nothing to test Thy power, but to the contrary to obtain knowledge of hidden things by the very holy virtue of Adonay whose power and kingdom will have no end in all the Ages of Ages. Amen.[84]

The conjuror next faces the direction of the triangle and recites a prayer to the appropriate planetary archangel. (See Appendix V for these prayers).

Perform Conjuration of the Planetary Intelligence and Engage

Still facing the direction of the triangle, the conjuror recites the conjuration of the Planetary Intelligence (see Appendix VI for the conjurations). It is important to be aware that you may need to repeat the conjuration several times. If the spirit does not attend after the first recitation of the conjuration, repeat it. The conjuration should be spoken in a clear, firm, and steady voice.

---

84 See *Key of Solomon*. Skinner & Rankine, 2008:292.

When the seer confirms spirit contact,[85] the conjuror should test the spirit. Conjuration can draw the attention of other spirits as well as the one you are seeking to connect with, who are not necessarily friendly.

The conjuror asks:

Are you the same Intelligence, whom we have moved & called forth to visible appearance here before us at this time, known by the name (N)?

If the spirit does not answer, repeat the question. If it says yes, ask it to affirm its identity by proclaiming the divine names Jahveh, Adonay, Eheieh, and Agla and its own name. If the spirit refuses, or changes form on saying the names, it is not the Intelligence you want. At this point you may feel it is appropriate to do a banishing, and restart from the first prayer to God.

If the Intelligence confirms its identity, the conjuror should welcome it:

Welcome Intelligence by the light of the Highest, we thank you for your attendance and ask for your assistance in this rite in the name of our Lord God, whose name be glorified both now and forever. Amen.[86]

From the wording of the conjuration it is phrased so that if the Intelligence is busy it will send one of its servant spirits to act in its place. If this is the case the spirit is likely to identify itself as a servant of the Intelligence, and should be asked for its name and still tested as above. You should also at this point carry out the procedure mentioned in Appendix II of drawing up the seal using Aiq Beker to ensure you have the correct seal for the spirit.

The conjuror asks the questions prepared beforehand. After each question the conjuror should wait for the skryer to receive a response from the Intelligence, and then to relay that response for the scribe (or conjuror if there is no scribe) to record. The questions should have been carefully considered and worded so there is no ambiguity in them. One of the questions should be if there is anything the Intelligence would prefer done differently for future contact, or if it can be simplified. If you request a familiar spirit from the Intelligence, make this the last question,

---

85 This may often appear with a vision as the clearing of mist or a parting of a veil.

86 Based on the welcome in *Janua Magica Reserata*. Skinner & Rankine, 2005:126.

and on hearing the name the Intelligence gives, work out the seal based on how you have transliterated the name, and ask the Intelligence if this is the correct seal for the said spirit.[87] If it is not, check your transliteration and try again.[88] Also ask if the same method of contact should be used for this spirit or if there is another method or differences in how the communication should be conducted.

If you ask the Intelligence to perform a task, be very precise, give it a timeframe to perform the task in, and ask it to take an oath in the name of God that it will carry out the task. (So something like: '[N] I ask that you perform this task [detail of task] in the next [timeframe] in the Name and Service of our Lord the Most High God.') Tasks can also include requesting that the Intelligence charge a talisman or amulet placed under the crystal in the triangle at the beginning.

GIVE LICENSE TO DEPART AND END RITE

The conjuror then gives the license to depart:[89]

> *O thou Spirit N: because you have very diligently answered our demands, & were very willing to come at our (first) Call, We do here Licence you and any other spirits present to depart to your proper place, without doing any harm, injury or danger to Man or Beast or place (depart I say) & be ever ready to come at our Call, being conjured by the sacred rites of magic, We charge thee to depart peaceably & quietly, and the Peace of God be ever continued between us & thee. Amen.*[90]

All should then in silence (to avoid cross-contamination of perceptions) record any impressions and feelings they had, phenomena they experienced, etc., during the rite. If the conjuror and others feel satisfied the Intelligence has left and there are no other presences, the magic circle may be opened

---

87 'It is also Concluded & Certainly Affirmed, that Every Star in the firmament hath its particular governing Intelligence, or Angelical spirit appropriate to it: with their Several & Respective Servient powers also, as a Militia under Each of them, not further to be named singly being numberless.' Skinner & Rankine, 2005:98.

88 If you intend to ask for a familiar spirit, be sure you have some paper with the appropriate planetary kamea on so you can use them to work out the seal of the spirit's name. See Appendix II.

89 Note I amended this license so it includes any other spirits attracted.

90 Adapted from license to depart in *Book of Treasure Spirits*. Rankine, 2009:80.

and all depart. If anyone present feels at all uneasy or uncertain at this point, perform a banishing before opening the circle.

As all the participants are likely to be hungry, and may be tired or hyped, they should now eat and drink to help return themselves to a more normal state.

AFTERWORD

Sometimes, for no obvious reason, a conjuration does not appear to work, even when everything seems to have been done correctly. This could be because the spirit is otherwise occupied, or something was missed. This is not cause for being disheartened; conjuration does not have a guaranteed 100% success rate. In such instances check through your records and assess if there is anything that can be improved, choose a suitable date and perform the conjuration again. If the contact does not occur after repeated conjurations, make a dream charm if you do not already have one and use it for a week after the conjuration (see Appendix VII).

Another consideration is that sometimes it seems like nothing has happened, and then you get the answers you were looking for in a dream. Spirit communication in dreams is not uncommon, as it is an easier interface for contact between them and us. As such it is particularly important to record your dreams in the run-up to a conjuration, and in the days following.

Final Message

It is my fervent hope that you have great success in your conjurations with this material. I also hope that it provides a firm foundation for further conjurations and work with whichever grimoires you are drawn to. The template here will work as a skeleton, to which can be added material unique to the grimoire you choose. Each different grimoire has different things to offer, and will require more focus on different areas, e.g. a lot more prayer sequences (*Sworn Book of Honorius*), more complex and variable magic circles (*Heptameron*), a specific set of tools with their consecrations (*Grimorium Verum*), etc. This material should prepare you well for ventures into such works. Remember, **planning**, **preparation**, and **purification**. And treat all spirits with respect!

APPENDIX I: Planetary Days & Hours

Timing is an important consideration when performing work with the seven classical planets and choosing a favourable time to perform your ceremony is a key factor in securing effective results for your magic.

In order to decide which planetary day or hours to perform your magic in you need to consider the nature of the results you require so that you will be able to select the most auspicious day and time at which to perform it. Each of the days of the week are associated with one of the classical planets and for this reason it is preferable to perform your ceremony on the day associated with the planetary energy most relevant to your ceremony. When invoking a planetary spirit you would do so on the day of the planet it is associated with, or if you were consecrating a talisman or amulet you would use the day of the week corresponding to the energy you wish to charge it with.

Whichever planet you are working with, in addition to performing your ceremony on the day of the week associated with that planet, it is preferable to also use one of the hours on that day (or night) associated with the planet. If you need to perform a ceremony urgently and it is not practical to wait for the planetary day, you can still use the planetary hours of the planet on any day of the week to tune in to the energies of that planet.

Likewise if a ceremony is for an intent which falls under the influence of two planets, their influence can be combined by using the planetary hour of one of the planets on the planctary day of the other planet. E.g., if you were performing a ceremony for career success, you would notice that this is something which benefits from the influence of both Jupiter and the Sun. Therefore you could tap into the energy of both these planets by either performing your ceremony during a solar hour on Thursday, or a Jupiterian hour on a Sunday.

Planetary Days

The popular sequence of planetary attributions of the days comes from ancient Mesopotamia. This was subsequently adopted by the Greeks, who attributed their deities to the days in accordance with similarities between the qualities and attributes of their deities with the earlier Mesopotamian ones. The Romans then followed the same procedure, replacing the Greek deities with their Roman equivalents. Thus it was that the familiar sequence of Sun, Moon, Mars, Mercury, Jupiter, Venus, and Saturn for the days was established with the Roman deities (with the subsequent inclusion of Germanic/Norse deities), i.e. Sunday, Monday, Tuesday, Wednesday, Thursday, Friday, and Saturday.

Planetary Hours

I will speak of the unequal hours which are attributed unto the dominion or rule of the planets, for that the dominion of the hour serveth to the planets as for a dignity.[91]

Although the idea that working with planetary hours has been promoted by some people as starting with the medieval grimoires, this is not the case. In ancient Egypt the Egyptian priests attributed a different ruling god to each of the twenty-four hours of the day. The Greeks adopted this idea, rationalising it into the system that we are familiar with. They attributed the seven planets to the hours of the day[92] and through this they developed the system in which the repetitive sequence of the seven planets was first introduced.

If you are new to the concept of planetary hours you may at first be overwhelmed by the confusing use of the term 'hour' for each time period as these are not the sixty-minute hours that we are accustomed to using in normal timekeeping. The planetary days are divided into twenty-four planetary hours starting with the first hour of the day beginning at sunrise and ending with the last hour of the day ending at sunrise of the next planetary day.

The period of daylight that extends from sunrise to sunset is divided into the twelve 'hours' of the day. The period of darkness extending from sunset to sunrise of the next day is divided into the twelve 'hours' of night.

---

91 *A Brief and most Easy Astrological Judgment of the Stars*, Claudius Dariot, 1583.
92 See *The Exact Sciences in Antiquity*, Neugebauer, 1967:169.

Combined, these give the twenty-four hours of the planetary day. As the duration of daylight and darkness varies except at the Spring and Autumn Equinoxes, on a particular planetary day the length of the hours of the day will differ from the length of the hours of the night. This is why the planetary hours are sometimes called the unequal hours. During the *'light'* half of the year between the Spring and Autumn Equinoxes there will be more hours of daylight than night, so the twelve planetary hours of the day will be longer than the twelve planetary hours of the night. The converse is true during the *'dark'* half of the year between the Autumn and Spring Equinoxes, when there are more hours of darkness than daylight and so correspondingly the twelve planetary hours of night are longer than those of the day.

Almanacs, ephemerides and the internet are all sources you can use to discover the sunrise and sunset times, enabling you to calculate the planetary hours in advance and time your ceremonies appropriately.

ATTRIBUTIONS FOR PLANETARY HOURS

Hour	*Planetary Hours of the Day*						
	Sun.	Mon.	Tues.	Wed.	Thurs.	Fri.	Sat.
1	Sun (☉)	☽	♂	☿	♃	♀	♄
2	Venus (♀)	♄	☉	☽	♂	☿	♃
3	Mercury (☿)	♃	♀	♄	☉	☽	♂
4	Moon (☽)	♂	☿	♃	♀	♄	☉
5	Saturn (♄)	☉	☽	♂	☿	♃	♀
6	Jupiter (♃)	♀	♄	☉	☽	♂	☿
7	Mars (♂)	☿	♃	♀	♄	☉	☽
8	Sun (☉)	☽	♂	☿	♃	♀	♄
9	Venus (♀)	♄	☉	☽	♂	☿	♃
10	Mercury (☿)	♃	♀	♄	☉	☽	♂
11	Moon (☽)	♂	☿	♃	♀	♄	☉
12	Saturn (♄)	☉	☽	♂	☿	♃	♀

			Planetary Hours of the Night				
Hour	Sun.	Mon.	Tues.	Wed.	Thurs.	Fri.	Sat.
1	Jupiter (♃)	♀	♄	☉	☽	♂	☿
2	Mars (♂)	☿	♃	♀	♄	☉	☽
3	Sun (☉)	☽	♂	☿	♃	♀	♄
4	Venus (♀)	♄	☉	☽	♂	☿	♃
5	Mercury (☿)	♃	♀	♄	☉	☽	♂
6	Moon (☽)	♂	☿	♃	♀	♄	☉
7	Saturn (♄)	☉	☽	♂	☿	♃	♀
8	Jupiter (♃)	♀	♄	☉	☽	♂	☿
9	Mars (♂)	☿	♃	♀	♄	☉	☽
10	Sun (☉)	☽	♂	☿	♃	♀	♄
11	Venus (♀)	♄	☉	☽	♂	☿	♃
12	Mercury (☿)	♃	♀	♄	☉	☽	♂

CALCULATIONS: EXAMPLE 1

Let us say you wanted to work out the planetary hours for a ritual that focused on using Mercurial energies. Wednesday is the day of Mercury, so you decide to perform the ritual next Wednesday, during the day. The process is then as follows:

- Consulting an almanac you see the sun rises at 7am on that day and sets at 8.48pm.
- So the hours of daylight are from 07.00 – 20:48, giving 13 hours and 48 minutes.
- 13 x 60 + 48 = 828 minutes of daylight.
- Divide by 12 = 69.
- This means each of the 12 'hours' of daylight will be 69 minutes long.

Consulting the tables given you see the first and eighth hours of Wednesday are ruled by Mercury. So for the first hour of the day the ritual should be performed between 7.00am and 8.09am (69 minutes).

For the eighth hour further calculation is needed:

- Add together the 'hours' length for 7 'hours' (7 x 69 = 483 minutes, or 8 hours and 3 minutes).
- Then add this to the sunrise time (7:00am) + 8 hours and 3 minutes = 3:03pm).
- This means the eighth hour starts at 3:03pm and finishes at 4:12pm (3:03 + 69 minutes).

You then decide which of these two times will be more practical, and you have your time to perform the ritual in.

Calculations: Example 2

Let us say you now wanted to work out the planetary hours for a ritual that focused on using Saturnian energies. Saturday is the day of Saturn, so you decide to perform the ritual next Saturday, during the night when Saturn is visible in the sky. The process is then as follows:

- Consulting an almanac you see the sun sets at 9.04pm on that day and rises the following morning at 6.10am.
- So the hours of night are from 21.04 – 06:10, giving 9 hours and 6 minutes.
- 9 x 60 + 6 = 546 minutes of night.
- Divide by 12 = 45.5.
- This means each of the 12 'hours' of the night will be 45.5 minutes long.

Consulting the tables given you see the third and tenth hours of Saturday night are ruled by Saturn. So if you now calculate these two times you have your options. For the third hour:

- Sunset is 9.04pm so this is the base time you start from.
- To calculate the start time for the third hour, add the 'hours' length for 2 'hours' (2 x 45.5 = 91 minutes, or 1 hour and 31 minutes)
- Add this to the sunset time (9.04) + 1 hour and 31 minutes = 10.35pm

- The Saturnian hour runs from 10.35pm to 11.20.5pm (10.35 + 45.5 minutes)

For the tenth hour further calculation is needed:

- Add together the 'hours' length for 9 'hours' (9 x 45.5 = 409.5 minutes, or 6 hours and 49.5 minutes).
- Then add this to the sunset time (9:04pm) + 6 hours and 49.5 minutes = 3:53.5am).
- This means the tenth hour starts at 3:53.5am and finishes at 4:39am (3:53.5 + 45.5 minutes).

You then decide which of these two times will be more practical (probably 10.35pm!), and you have your time to perform the ritual in.

One further aspect you may wish to consider is the planetary movement. At times some of the planets go retrograde, i.e. appear to reverse their movement in the sky. This is taken in magical terms to mean the energy is waning rather than waxing, so many magicians prefer to work when the planet is not retrograde. This can easily be checked by looking at an Astrological Ephemeris.

APPENDIX II: Sigil Construction using Aiq Beker

Aiq Beker

A SIGIL is a pictographic representation of the name of a spiritual creature or of your intent. When you use a sigil representing a spiritual creature you are creating a gateway for the energy of that creature to manifest. When you draw a sigil of this sort onto an amulet or talisman, you are creating a link to the spiritual creature to enable energy to be drawn from it, like charge from a battery.

The standard method of creating sigils on the kameas uses Hebrew letters, based on what is called Aiq Beker or the Qabalah of Nine Chambers (this takes its name from the letters attributed to the first two numbers, i.e. Aleph, Yod, Qoph to 1 – AIQ, then Beth, Kaph, Resh to 2 – BKR). This system reduces the numbers attributed to the letters to a numerical value in the range 1-9, ignoring the zeros of tens and hundreds.

The *Qabalah of Nine Chambers*

1	2	3
Aleph (1)	Beth (2)	Gimel (3)
Yod (10)	Kaph (20)	Lamed (30)
Qoph (100)	Resh (200)	Shin (300)
4	5	6
Daleth (4)	Heh (5)	Vav (6)
Mem (40)	Nun (50)	Samekh (60)
Tav (400)	Final Kaph (500)	Final Mem (600)
7	8	9
Zain (7)	Cheth (8)	Teth (9)
Ayin (70)	Peh (80)	Tzaddi (90)
Final Nun (700)	Final Peh (800)	Final Tzaddi (900)

Hebrew words are used on kameas, the sigil being formed by drawing lines joining the squares corresponding to the numerical values of the letters in sequence. The numbers attributed to the letters are used according to the range of numbers within the kamea. If the letter has a higher number attributed to it than exists in the kamea, the number is dropped to the highest number available in the Aiq Beker table. As the largest kamea is that of the Moon, which has the number range 1-81, any letter with a numerical value over 80 will always be reduced. Therefore 90 (Tzaddi) will always be reduced to 9 but 100 (Qoph) will drop to 10 unless it is in the Saturnian kamea with a range of 1-9, where it would drop to 1. To clarify:

Letter	Numerical Value	Not Reduced in
Yod	10	4x4 (Jupiter) onwards
Kaph	20	5x5 (Mars) onwards
Lamed	30	6x6 (Sun) onwards
Mem	40	7x7 (Venus) onwards
Nun	50	8x8 (Mercury) onwards
Samekh	60	8x8 (Mercury) onwards
Ayin	70	9x9 (Moon) onwards
Peh	80	9x9 (Moon) onwards
		Drops a 0
Tzaddi	90	In all
Qoph	100	In all except 3x3 (Saturn) drops 2 0's
Resh	200	In all except 4x4 (Jupiter) and below when drops 2 0's
Shin	300	In all except 5x5 (Mars) and below when drops 2 0's
Tav	400	In all except 6x6 (Sun) and below when drops 2 0's

The first step in creating the sigil is to take the word and reduce it to a sequence of numbers, as attributed in the Qabalah of Nine Chambers.

The sigil is always begun with a small circle in the middle of the square containing the number that the first letter is attributed to. This is joined by a straight line to the middle of the square the number attributed to the next letter is in. This process is repeated until the line is drawn to the middle of the square containing the number to which the last letter is attributed, where a small circle is drawn to end the sigil.[93] This method hence only uses the squares containing the numbers 1-9, and sometimes numbers which are multiples of 10. The rest of the squares in the kamea are ignored.

---

93 Some sources have a small cross-bar at the end, but circles at both ends for the Intelligences makes them feel more connected to the planetary seals which have a lot of circle-ended lines in them.

If two consecutive letters are attributed to the same number, and hence the same box in the kamea, this is indicated by a small loop (U-shape) before continuing as a straight line to the box containing the number attributed to the next letter. If a third or fourth letter were also attributed to the same box, an extra loop would be added for each extra letter in the word that has the same numerical attribution.

Here are two examples of this technique:

Azrael is written AZRAL in Hebrew.
A + Z + R + A + L
1 + 7 + 200 + 1 + 30

Using Aiq Beker, the zeroes are removed from the R (200 becomes 2 because on Saturn kamea with number range of 1-9) and the L (30 becomes 3 for same reason), giving the numerical sequence 1 – 7 – 2 – 1 – 3

If we now draw this on the Saturn kamea, we get the following sigil.

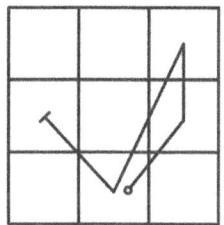

If however we were to draw the sigil for a word where there is more than one consecutive number of the same value, such as Satariel, the Kabbalistic Qliphoth of Binah, it would give the sequence 6 – 1 – 4 – 1 – 2 – 1 – 1 – 3, i.e. Samekh = 6(0), Aleph = 1, Tav = 4(00), Aleph = 1, Resh = 2(00), Yod = 1(0), Aleph = 1, Lamed = 3(0).

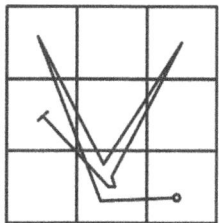

The Planetary Kameas

The kameas are magic squares, i.e. the rows, columns, and diagonals all add up to the same total. The row/column size is the primary number associated with the planet, e.g. 3 for Saturn (3x3) or 4 for Jupiter (4x4). The number of squares in each square, the row/column total and the square total are also numbers associated with the associated planet. Words such as divine names which add up to these totals are often used in talismans, e.g. Din (DIN) and Doni (DNI) both add to 64 and are used on Mercurial talismans.

Saturn – 3x3
Squares – 9; Row/Column/Diagonal total – 15; Square total – 45

4	9	2
3	5	7
8	1	6

Jupiter – 4x4
Squares – 16; Row/Column/Diagonal total – 34; Square total – 136

4	14	15	1
9	7	6	12
6	11	10	8
16	2	3	13

Mars – 5x5

Squares – 25; Row/Column/Diagonal total – 65; Square total – 325

11	24	7	20	3
4	12	25	8	16
17	5	13	21	9
10	18	1	14	22
23	6	19	2	15

Sun – 6x6

Squares – 36; Row/Column/Diagonal total – 111; Square total – 666

6	32	3	34	35	1
7	11	27	28	6	30
19	14	16	15	23	24
18	20	22	21	17	13
25	29	10	9	26	12
36	5	33	4	2	31

VENUS – 7x7

Squares – 49; Row/Column/Diagonal total – 175; Square total – 1225

22	47	16	41	10	35	4
5	23	48	17	42	11	29
30	6	24	49	18	36	12
13	31	7	25	43	19	37
38	14	32	1	26	44	20
21	39	8	33	2	27	45
46	15	40	9	34	3	28

MERCURY – 8x8

Squares – 64; Row/Column/Diagonal total – 260; Square total – 2080

8	58	59	5	4	62	63	1
49	15	14	52	53	11	10	56
41	23	22	44	46	19	18	45
32	34	36	29	25	38	39	28
40	26	27	37	36	30	31	33
17	47	46	20	21	43	42	24
9	55	54	12	13	51	50	16
64	2	3	61	60	6	7	57

Moon – 9x9

Squares – 81; Row/Column/Diagonal total – 369; Square total – 3321

37	78	29	70	21	62	13	54	5
6	38	79	30	71	22	63	14	46
47	7	39	80	31	72	23	55	15
16	48	8	40	81	32	64	24	56
57	17	49	9	41	73	33	65	25
26	58	18	50	1	42	74	34	66
67	27	59	10	51	2	43	75	35
36	68	19	60	11	52	3	44	76
77	28	69	20	61	12	53	4	45

APPENDIX III: Images of the Sigils and Seals

This appendix contains the sigils of the Planetary Intelligences on their appropriate planetary kameas, followed by the Planetary Seal. I have provided two versions of each sigil, one of which will look different to those you may have seen previously online or in books. This is because I have drawn them following the rules of Aiq Beker, and Agrippa did not completely follow these rules. Strictly speaking Agrippa drew the sigils incorrectly, not always reducing the minimum level, and had a habit of merging IA to 11 rather than two separate points at 10 and 1.[94]

As Agrippa was seen as the authority, nobody ever questioned his depictions of the sigils,[95] and they have been reproduced ever since in his forms. This raises an interesting issue, because over the centuries people (myself included) have used these 'incorrect' forms and still achieved successful conjuration of the Intelligences. This then leaves us with interesting possibilities, such as the Intelligences accepting the Agrippa version of the sigil as a contact point because everybody used it, or that the sigil is of less importance than the conjuration itself and other details in achieving success (i.e. the magical momentum).

What is clear is that the Agrippa version has been used extensively and works, and the correctly drawn sigils also work, so it is up to you which one you choose to use for your conjuration.

---

94 For more details describing all of the incorrect attributions including the Planetary Spirits, see my essay 'Agrippa & the Magic Squares', at my website www.davidrankine.com.

95 There is an important message in this, which is even authorities can make mistakes and you should not be afraid to question information, check it, and validate it.

Agiel

Agrippa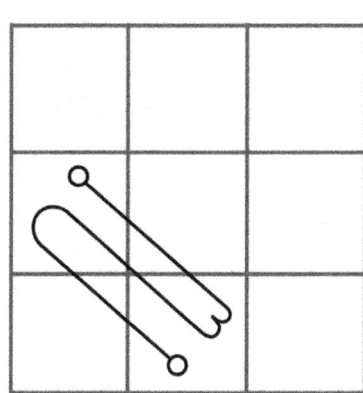

Corrected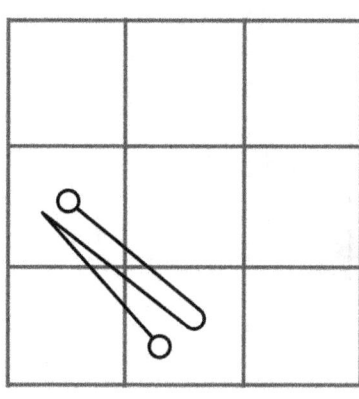

Loop where it should be sharp
Double loop where it should be single loop

$1 + 3 + 1(0) + 1 + 3(0)$

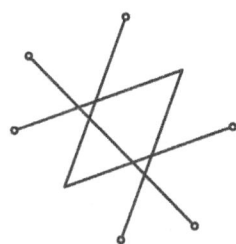

Johphiel

Agrippa	Corrected
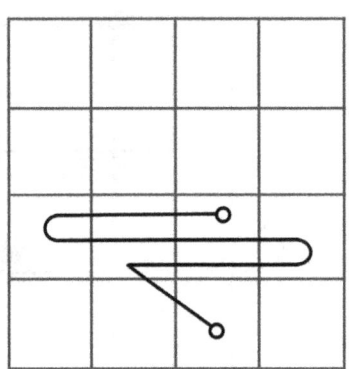	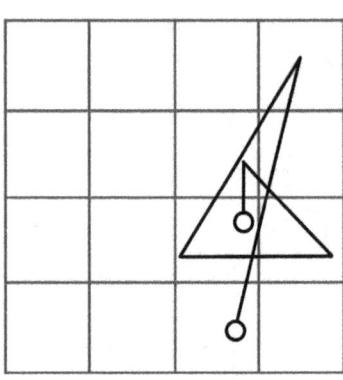
Second point goes to 5 (Heh) rather than 6 (Vav). Second point is loop instead of sharp Third point is loop instead of sharp Combines I+A so sigil goes to 11 instead of 10 + 1	10 + 6 + 8(0) + 10 + 1 + 3(0)

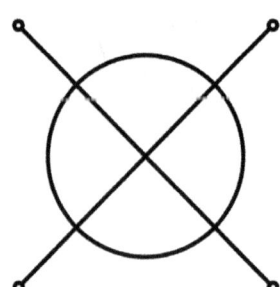

GRAPHIEL

Agrippa	Corrected
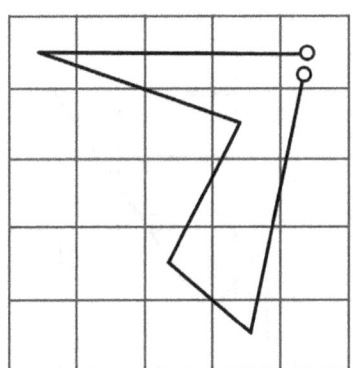	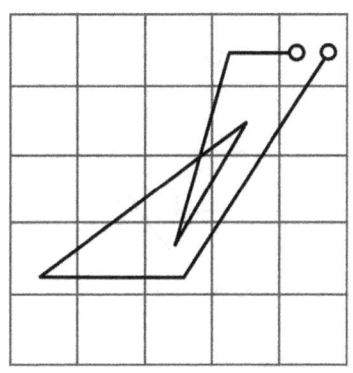

Second letter is reduced to 2 instead of 20 so second point in wrong square
I+A combined to give 11 again instead of 10+1

$3 + 20(0) + 1 + 8(0) + 10 + 1 + 3(0)$

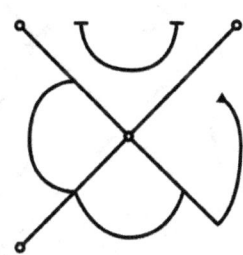

Nachiel

Agrippa

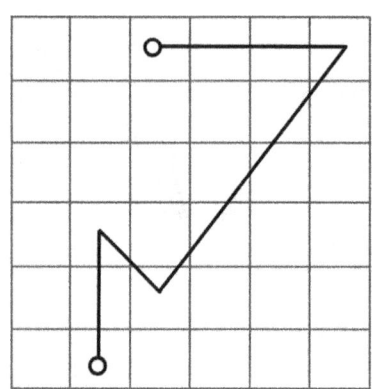

Reduces L from 30 to 3 so sigil ends in wrong square
Note I and A not combined this time

Corrected

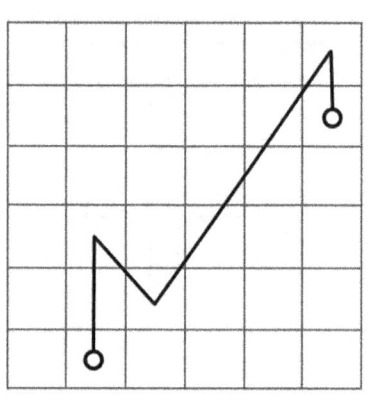

5(0) + 20 + 10 + 1 + 30

Hagiel

Agrippa

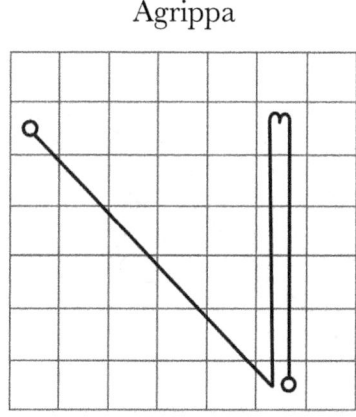

I+A combined again and represented as a double loop instead of sharp end, implying 3 letters of same value L reduced from 30 to 3 so wrong end point

Corrected

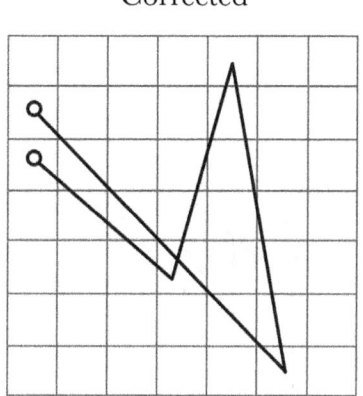

5 + 3 + 10 + 1 + 30

Tiriel

Agrippa	Corrected
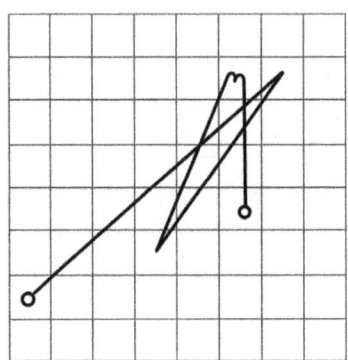	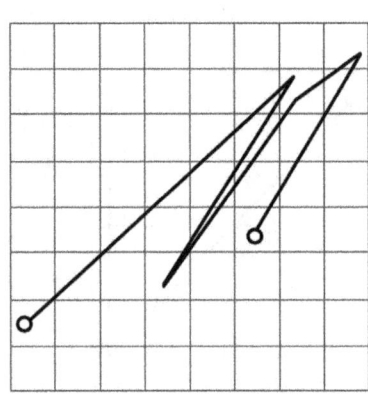
I+A combined to give 11 again instead of 10+1 and represented by a double loop which implies 3 letters of the same value. Note this time he does not reduce L(30)	9 + 10 + 20(0) + 10 + 1 + 30

Malcha

Agrippa

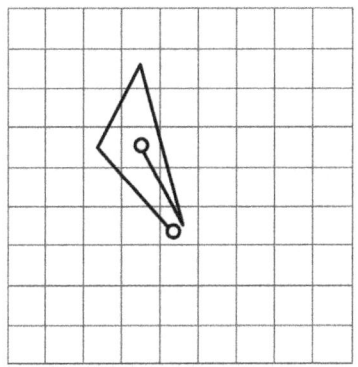

This would be correct if it was spelled MALCHA in Hebrew, but it is MLKA

Corrected

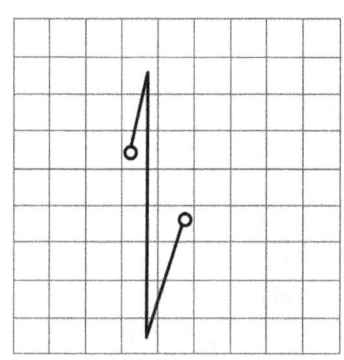

40 + 30 + 20 + 1

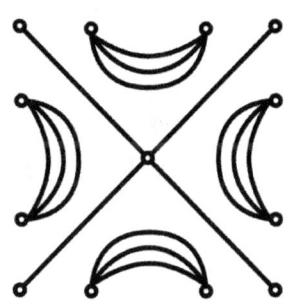

APPENDIX IV: Talisman/Seal/Lamen Construction

A LAMEN acts as a badge of recognition between you and the spirit. By wearing a lamen with the sigil of the spirit on it you are showing that spirit that you wish for a connection with it, and that you have respect for it. Everyone in the circle should have a lamen on. The lamen is worn over the heart pinned to the robe. On the front side should be a simple single band circle with the sigil of the Planetary Intelligence in it. On the reverse the same set-up but with the sigil of the planetary archangel instead. The archangel is then facing your heart, placing it in a position of protection of your heart and you.[96]

The seal has the same front, but with simply the seal of the planet on the reverse. The seal is placed under the crystal or mirror in the triangle to facilitate contact. To use an analogy, if the conjurations were the rings of a telephone call, the seal under the crystal is the phone number, and the crystal is the telephone.

A talisman may include all of these components and other appropriate ones.[97] That is up to you to decide. It acts as a receptacle for the energy of the spirit called, in this case the Intelligence, to charge the talisman for the function it has been created for. Placing the talisman under the crystal, so it is in contact with the crystal which is acting as the portal for the Intelligence allows for it to more effectively charge the talisman then if it was somewhere else, like inside the circle which is designed to keep out all spirit energies.

---

[96] The same principle is used with thwarting or controlling angels, see e.g. *The Goetia of Dr Rudd*. If for some reason you were to conjure a Planetary Spirit (also called a Planetary Demon), you would have the seal of the Planetary Intelligence (also called a Planetary Angel) on the reverse, as the Intelligence governs the Spirit.

[97] I am assuming the reader will have knowledge of the creation of talismans rather than adding a whole section on it here. If not, there are some excellent books on making talismans available. Personally I would recommend *How to Make and Use Talismans* by Israel Regardie.

Consecration of Seal and Lamen

Before placing the seal or lamen into consecrated silk, say:

> *I beseech Thy Majesty most humbly, that this seal [/this talisman/these lamens] be consecrated by Thy power and be prepared in such a manner that it [/they] will obtain truth and strength against all spirits, by Thee, Most Holy Adonay from whom the Kingdom and Empire have no end!*[98]

Then wrap and place safely ready for use in the conjuration.

Consecration of Talisman

After you have made the talisman (in an appropriate planetary hour and day) to be placed in the triangle under the crystal or mirror, recite the following prayer over the seal:[99]

> *O Almighty Lord and everlasting God, by whose power both the heavens and the Earth with all things therein contained were made, by whose providence all things both in heaven & earth are governed Who gives virtue to every Creature, that thou has made as to plants, stones, herbs, & all for the use of man (who in Thee does live, move, & have his being) yea & to words, prayers, signs & sigils do give special virtues, & especially to Thy own great Names, for expelling of evil spirits & healing diseases, give Thy special blessing unto these sigils which in thy Name we do apply unto this thy Servant, let those virtues equal the virtue of Gideon's Sword that vanquished the Philistines, of Judith that cut off the Babylonian's head, the strength of Sampson's arms, the strength of David; let his prayers that made them (who bear a place in the Celestial Choir) be now heard in remembrance, & let our weak prayers, have access unto Thy throne of Grace, & so for prayer with Thy Sacred Majesty that these Sigils may receive that virtue from Thee, that was humbly supplicated at the making of them, and Let this Thy Servant find & feel the effectual workings of them, to the Recovering of health both of body & mind, & preserving from the Like or any other evil, both of body & mind hereafter, & grant this O merciful Father for Jesus Christ his Sake in whose blessed Name we do humbly & heartily beg it, of Thee, in that prayer which he has taught us.*

Then wrap and place safely ready for charging in the conjuration.

---

98 *Key of Solomon.* Skinner & Rankine, 2008: 304.
99 A Prayer before the putting of any Sigil. Sloane MSS 3822, folio 35, 1739?

APPENDIX V: Archangel Prayers

The following prayers are based on the conjurations in the *Heptameron*, with some minor changes made to them for consistency and flow. The seals are from *The Nine Keys* and are used on the reverse of the lamens.

Cassiel – Archangel of Saturn

I conjure and call upon you, **Cassiel,** *strong and powerful Angel; and by the name* **Adonay, Adonay, Adonay, Eie, Eie, Eie, Acim, Acim, Acim, Cados, Cados, Ina, Ima, Saday, Ja, Sar***, Lord and maker of the world, who rested on the seventh day: And by Him who of his good pleasure gave the same to be observed by the Children of Israel throughout their Generations, that they should thoroughly keep and sanctify the same, to have thereby a good reward in the world to come, and by the names of the Angels serving in the seventh host, before* **Boel***, a great Angel and powerful Prince; and by the name of his Star, which is Saturn; and by his holy Seal; and by the names before spoken, I Conjure upon thee,* **Cassiel***, who are chief ruler of the seventh day, which is the Sabbath day, that you assist me, and fulfil all my petitions, according to my will and desire, in my cause and business.*

Seal of Cassiel/Zaphkiel from Harley MS 6482 fo. 206[100]

---

100 Text in band: 'In hoc signo vinca' – 'In this sign I conquer' (Latin) in top left; אלהים – Elohim (Hebrew) in top right; אלוהים – Elohim (Hebrew) alternative spelling in bottom right. Elohim means Gods and is a divine name associated with Saturn.

SACHIEL – ARCHANGEL OF JUPITER

I conjure and call upon you, you holy Angel, and by the name **Cados, Cados, Cados, Eschereie, Eschereie, Eschereie, Hatim, Ya**, *strong founder of the worlds,* **Cantine, Jaym, Janic, Anic, Calbot, Sabbac, Berisay, Alnaym**: *and by the name* **Adonay**, *who created fishes, and creeping things in the waters, and birds upon the face of the earth, and flying towards Heaven, in the fifth day; and by the names of the Angels serving in the sixth host, before* **Pastor**, *a holy Angel, and a great and powerful Prince; and by the name of his Star, which is Jupiter, and by the name of his Seal, and by the name* **Adonay**, *the great God, creator of all things; and by the name of all Stars, and by their Power and Virtue, and by all the names aforesaid, I conjure thee,* **Sachiel** *a great Angel, who are chief ruler of Thursday; and by the name* **Adonay**, *the living and true God, that you assist me, and fulfil all my petitions, according to my will and desire, in my cause and business.*

Seal of Sachiel from Harley MS 6482 fo. 218[101]

---

[101] Text in band (all Hebrew) anticlockwise from top: אל – Al (divine name associated with Jupiter in Kabbalah); הסד – Chesed (Glory, Kabbalistic sphere of Jupiter); שחיאל – Sachiel; חשמלים – Chasmalim (Brilliant Ones, order of angels associated with Chesed/Jupiter).

Samael – Archangel of Mars

*I conjure and call upon you, you strong and holy Angel, by the name **Ya, Ya, Ya, He, He, He, Va, Hy, Hy, Ha, Ha, Va, Va, Va, An, An, An, Aie, Aie, Aie, El, Ay, Elibra, Eloim, Eloim**; and by the name* of that high God who made the dry land appear, and called it Earth, and brought forth herbs and trees out of the same, and sealed the same with His precious, honourable, fearful and holy name; and by the name of the Angels ruling in the fifth heaven, who serve **Acimoy**, *a great Angel, strong, powerful, and honourable; and by the name of his Star which is Mars, and by the names aforesaid, I conjure you thee* **Samael**, *who are a great Angel, and are chief ruler of Tuesday; and by the name* **Adonay**, *the living and true God, that you assist me, and fulfil all my petitions, according to my will and desire, in my cause and business.*

Seal of Samael from Harley MS 6482 fo. 229v[102]

---

102 Text in band from top anticlockwise (all Hebrew): אלוהים גבר – Elohim Gibor (Mighty Gods, divine name associated with Geburah/Mars); גבורה – Geburah (Strength, Kabbalistic sphere of Mars); שרפהים – Seraphim (Fiery Serpents, order of angels associated with Geburah/Mars).

Michael – Archangel of the Sun

*I conjure and call upon you, you strong and holy Angel of God, in the name **Adonay, Eye, Eye, Eya**, which is He who was, and is, and is to come, **Eye, Abray**; and in the name **Saday, Cados, Cados, Cados**, sitting on high upon the Cherubim; and by the great Name of God Himself, strong and powerful, who is exalted above all Heavens; **Eye Saray**, maker of the World, who created the World, the Heaven, the Earth, the Sea, and all that is in them in the first day, and sealed them with his holy Name **Phaa**; and by the name of the holy Angels, who rule in the fourth Heaven, and serve before the most mighty **Salamia**, an Angel great and honourable; and by the name of his Star, which is Sol; and by his Sign; and by the immense name of the living God, and by all the names aforesaid, I conjure you, **Michael**, O great Angel, who are chief Ruler of the Lords day; and by the name **Adonay**, who has created the world, and all that is therein, that you assist me, and fulfil all my petitions, according to my will and desire, in my cause and business.*

Seal of Michael from Harley MS 6482 fo. 241v[103]

---

103 Text in band from top anticlockwise (all Hebrew): אלוה – Eloah (Divine name associated with Tiphereth/Sun); מלחים – Malachim (Kings, order of angels associated with Tiphereth/Sun); פליאל – Peliel (a Solar angel); מיכאל – Michael; טיפהרת Tiphereth (Beauty, Kabbalistic sphere of the Sun). Text in circle וריאל –Uriel (archangel).

ANAEL – ARCHANGEL OF VENUS

*I conjure and call upon you, you strong Angel, holy and powerful; in the name **On**, **Hey**, **Heya**, **Ja**, **Je**, **Adonay**, **Saday**, and in the name **Saday**, who created four-footed beasts, and creeping things, and man in the sixth day, and gave to Adam power over all creatures; wherefore blessed be the name of the creator in his place: and by the name of the Angels serving in the third host, before **Dagiel**, a great Angel, and a strong and powerful prince; and by the name of the Star which is Venus, and by his Seal which is holy, and by all the names aforesaid, I Conjure upon thee, **Anael**, who are chief ruler the sixth day, that you assist me, and fulfil all my petitions, according to my will and desire, in my cause and business.*

Seal of Anael from Harley MS 6482 fo. 253v[104]

---

104 Text in band from top anticlockwise (all Hebrew): אדוני שבות – Adonay Sabaoth (Lord of Hosts, divine name of Netzach/Venus); אנאל – Anael; אלוהים – Elohim (Gods, also the order of angels of Netzach/Venus); נצאח – Netzach (Victory, Kabbalistic sphere of Venus).

Raphael – Archangel of Mercury

I conjure and call upon you, you strong and holy angel, good and powerful, in a strong name of fear and praise, **Ja, Adonay, Elohim, Saday, Saday, Saday; Eie, Eie, Eie; Asamie, Asamie;** *and in the name of* **Adonay**, *who has made the two great lights, and distinguished day from night for the benefit of His creatures; and by the names of all the discerning angels, governing openly in the second house before the great angel,* **Tetra**, *strong and powerful; and by the name of his star which is Mercury; and by the name of his seal, which is that of a powerful and honoured God; and I call upon you,* **Raphael**, *and by the names above mentioned, you great angel who presides over the fourth day: and by the holy name which is written in the front of Aaron, created the most high priest, and by the names of all the angels who are constant in the grace of Christ, and by the name and place of Ammaluim, that you assist me, and fulfil all my petitions, according to my will and desire, in my cause and business.*

Seal of Raphael from Harley MS 6482 fo. 265[105]

---

105 Text in band from top anticlockwise (all Hebrew except one word): Sabaoth אלוהים – Elohim Sabaoth (Gods of Hosts, divine name of Hod/Mercury, note Sabaoth in English); מיכאל – Michael (author may have bene hedging bets as Michael sometimes attributed to Mercury); ראפהאל – Raphael (archangel of Hod/Mercury); הוד – Hod (Splendour, sphere of Mercury in Kabbalah).

Gabriel – Archangel of the Moon

*I conjure and call upon you, you strong and good Angel, in the name **Adonay, Adonay, Adonay, Eye, Eye, Eye; Cados, Cados, Cados, Achim, Achim, Ja, Ja,** strong **Ja,** who appeared in Mount Sinai, with the glorification of **Adonay, Saday, Zebaoth, Anathay, Ya, Ya, Ya, Marinata, Abim, Jeia,** who created the Sea and all lakes and waters in the second day, which are above the Heavens and in the Earth, and sealed the Sea in His high name, and gave it bounds, beyond which it cannot pass: And by the names of the Angels, who rule in the first Legion, who serve **Orphaniel,** a great, precious and honourable Angel, and by the name of his Star, which is Luna; and by all the names aforesaid, I conjure thee, **Gabriel,** who are chief Ruler of Monday the second day; and by the name **Adonay,** who has created the world, and all that is therein, that you assist me, and fulfil all my petitions, according to my will and desire, in my cause and business.*

Seal of Gabriel from Harley MS 6482 fo. 277v[106]

---

106 Text in band from top anticlockwise (all Hebrew): סדאי אל חי – Shaddai El Chai (Almighty Everliving God, divine name of Yesod/the Moon; note has bad Hebrew transliteration/transcription); יסוד – Yesod (Foundation, Kabbalistic sphere of the Moon); גבריאל – Gabriel; מוריאל Muriel (lunar angel).

APPENDIX VI: Planetary Intelligence Conjurations

These conjurations were previously published in *Conjuring the Planetary Intelligences* (2019). Following discussion with several people who asked, I modernised the English and changed a few words for a better flow in the conjurations. Using the slightly revised conjurations worked well for myself and the other people I passed them on to. I have also removed the footnotes referring to minor textual differences as not being relevant to this work.

Note when a name is in bold this means it should be emphasised, i.e. intoned or vibrated.

Conjuration of Agiel

O You benevolent Intelligence, of Celestial light, Dignified, & by Nature Angelic, who are known or called by the name, **Agiel:** *& said to be of the nature & office, of the planet or star called Saturn, when by Celestial position it shall, be both well dignified, and fortified with all others your substitutes the president Intelligences, or dignified powers of Light residing in or otherwise appertaining to your Mansion, Orders or Hierarchy from the Superior to the Inferior and serving the most High God in your respective Orders & offices as Mediums of Divine Grace and Mercy, & as in Charge Command & Appointed we the Servants also of the Highest Reverently here present in his holy fear Do Earnestly, beseech humbly Request Strongly Invocate Call forth & powerfully move you to Visible Appearance in by & through these Excellent Ineffable great Signal Sacred & Divine Names of your God* **Ab: Hod, Jah: Hod:**[107] *Even the Omnipotent Immortal Immense Incomprehensible & most high god and Lord of hosts* **Jehovah,** *before whom the whole choir of heaven continually sings,* **O Mappa:laman Hallelujah** *And by the Seal of your Creation being the Mark or Character of holiness unto you & by the great Mystery Virtue force power Efficacy and Influence, of all we Do Strongly Invocate Confidently Call forth & powerfully Move you O you Benevolent Intelligence or Angelical Medium of Light Celestially Dignified who by name are Called* **Agiel** *with all Others the president & Servient Angels or Mediums of Light Celestially Dignified by Degree & office in general & particular Every & Each one for & by itself respectively appertaining to your Hierarchy mansion or place of residence to Visible Appearance; move therefore O ye Benevolent Intelligence,* **Agiel,** *with all Others of your Orders office Hierarchy Or Mansion Jointly & Severally as aforesaid gird up & gather your Self or Selves Accordingly together & some one or more of you, as it shall please God of his Special grace & permission is given to you and also Accordingly Descend from your Mansion or place of Residence or wheresoever Else you may be Otherwise officiating or Chancely Absent therefrom and Immediately forthwith Appear Visibly, here before us in this Crystal Stone*[108] *standing here before us and in and through the same to transmit your true and real presence In Splendid Appearance plainly unto the Light of our Eyes Utter your Voices unto our Ears that we may Not only Visibly see you but Audibly hear you Speak unto us and that we may Converse with*

---

107 The divine names associated with the Saturn kamea are Ab, Hod, Jah, Hod, probably here representing an expansion of AHIH ('I am', divine name of Kether).

108 Replace with mirror or glass receptacle if using either of these rather than a crystal. This is the same for all conjurations.

*you or otherwise forthwith Appear out of them Visible Upon this Triangle or Hereby upon the floor and Show plainly & visibly unto us A Sufficient Sign or test of your Coming and Appearance therefore we Do Entreat you and Undeniably Request you Charge Constrain Command and powerfully Move you O you Royal and Amicable Angel or Blessed Intelligence **Agiel** who art lately Ascribed to the planet **Saturn** and by the great Names of god governing that planet: **Ab: Hod: Jah: Hod: Jehovah:** God again and again powerfully without any delay Lingering or tarrying strictly charge that you descend Not one Minute Longer to Serve us and really fulfil all that is appropriated and belonging to your Charge Under the planet: **Saturn: Agiel: Agiel: Agiel:** gird up Move Come forth and faithfully Answer to all that belongs to your Hierarchy office or order I being Armed with power from above **Agiel:** behold the Exorcism the Stamp of the very Idea the Microcosm: by: **Agla: El: On: Tetragrammaton:** by: **Ogim Osj** who Sitteth Upon the throne by all that hath been Now is and Ever Shall be by the patriarchs and prophets by the Great lamen **Shemhamphorash** by heaven Earth and hell **Agiel** thou blessed Intelligence of **Saturn** by All Aforesaid: Move: Move: Move: Come forth and Visibly Show yourself at this Very Minute as you will answer the Contrary being high Misdemeanour at your peril before him who Shall Come to Judge the quick and the Dead and the world by fire fiat fiat fiat for why we are Servants of the same your god, and true worshippers of the Highest, wherefore be friendly unto us and Do for us as for the Servants of the Highest whereunto In his Name we Do again Earnestly Request elegantly and undeniably Move you both in power and presence O you Royal Spirit **Agiel** whose friendship unto us herein and works Shall be a Song of honour and the praise of God in His Creation. Amen.*

Conjuration of Johphiel

*O You benevolent Intelligence of Celestial Light Dignified and by Nature Angelic who are Known or Called by the name **Johphiel** & Said to be of the Nature & office of the planet or Star called Jupiter when by Celestial position it Shall be both Essentially & well Dignified and fortified with all others your Substitutes the president Intelligences or Dignified powers of Light properly Residing in or otherwise Appertaining to your Mansion orders or Hierarchy from the Superior to the Inferior & Serving the most high God in your Respective orders and office as Mediums of Divine Grace and Mercy and as in Charge Commanded & appointed we the servants Also of the Highest Reverently here present in his holy fear do Earnestly beseech humbly request strongly Invocate Call forth & powerfully Move you to Visible Appearance in by & through these Excellent Ineffable great Signal Sacred and Divine Names of your god:* **El: Ab: Aba:** *Even the Omnipotent Immortal Immense Incomprehensible and most high god & Lord of hosts Jehovah before whom the whole choir of heaven continually sings:* **O Mappa Laman: Hallelujah** *and by the seal of your Creation being the Mark or Character of holiness unto you and by the great Mystery virtue force and power Efficacy & Influence of all we Do Strongly Invocate Confidently Call forth and powerfully Move you O you benevolent Intelligence or Angelical Mediums of Light Celestially Dignified who by name are Called **Johphiel**: with all others the president & Servient Angels or Mediums of Light Celestially dignified by degree & office in general & particular Every and Each one for and by it Self Respectively Appertaining to your Hierarchy Mansion or place of Residence to Visible appearance Move therefore O you Benevolent Intelligence **Johphiel**: with all others of your orders office Hierarchy or Mansion Jointly and Severally as aforesaid: gird up & gather your Self or Selves accordingly together & Some one or Either more of you as it Shall please god of his Special grace & permission is given to you & also Accordingly Descend from your Mansion or place of Residence or wheresoever Else you may Be otherwise officiating or Chancely absent therefrom & Immediately forthwith Appear Visibly here before us in this Crystal Stone standing here before us & in & through the Same to transmit your true and Real presence In Splendid Appearance plainly unto the Sight of our Eyes Utter your Voices Unto our Ears, that we May Not only Visible See you but Audibly hear you Speak unto us and that we may Converse with you or otherwise forthwith Appear out of them visibly upon this triangle or fairly Upon the floor and Show plainly & visibly unto us a Sufficient Sign or test of your Coming and Appearance therefore we Do Entreat you and Undeniably Request you Charge Constrain Command and powerfully Move you O you Royal and Amicable Angel or blessed Intelligence **Johphiel** who art truly Ascribed to the planet Jupiter and* by the great Names of god governing that planet: **El: Ab: Aba: Jehovah:** I do again and again powerfully without any delay Lingering or Tarrying: Strictly Charge that you Defer Not one Minute Longer to Serve Us and Really fulfil all that is Appreciated and Belonging to your Charge under the planet Jupiter **Johphiel: Johphiel: Johphiel** gird up Move Come forth and faithfully Answer to all that belongs to your Hierarchy office or order I being armed with power from above **Johphiel** behold the Exorcist the stamp of the very Idea the Microcosm by **Agla: El: On: Tetragrammaton** by **Ogim Osj** who Sitteth upon the Throne by all that hath been Now is and Ever Shall be by the patriarchs and prophets by the great banner **Shemhamphorash** by heaven earth hell **Johphiel** thou Blessed Intelligence of Jupiter by all aforesaid Move Move Move Come forth and Visibly Show thy Self at this very Minute as you will Answer the Contrary being high Misdemeanour at your peril before him Who shall Come to Judge the quick and the dead and the World by fire, fiat: fiat: fiat for why we are Servants of the Same your god and true Worshippers of the highest wherefore be friendly unto us and Do for us as for the Servants of the highest whereunto for his Name we do again Earnestly Request urgently and Undeniably Move you both in power and presence O you Royal Spirit **Johphiel** whose friendship unto us herein and works Shall be a Song of honour and praise of God in His Creation Amen.

Conjuration of Graphiel

O You benevolent Intelligence of Celestial Light dignified and by Nature Angelic who are known or called by the name **Graphiel** *and said to be of the nature and office of the planet or star called Mars when by celestial position it shall be both essentially well dignified and fortified with all others your substitutes the president Intelligences or dignified powers of Light properly residing in or otherwise appertaining to your mansion orders hierarchy from the Superior to the Inferior and serving the Most High God in your respective orders and office as Mediums of Divine Grace and Mercy and as in charge commanded and appointed, we the servants also of the Highest reverentially here present in His holy fear do earnestly beseech humbly request strongly invocate call forth and powerfully move you to Visible Appearance in by and through these Excellent Ineffable great Signal Sacred & Divine Names of our God:* **Adonay: Melech: Ehejah:** *even the Omnipotent Immortal Immense Incomprehensible and Most High God and Lord of Hosts:* **Jehovah:** *before whom the whole choir of heaven continually sings:* **O Mappa Laman Hallelujah** *and by the seal of your Creation being the Mark of Character of holiness unto you and by the great mystery virtue force and power efficacy and influence of all we do strongly invocate confidently call forth and powerfully move you O you benevolent Intelligence or Angelic Mediums of Light celestially dignified who by Name is called* **Graphiel** *with all others the president and servient Angels or Mediums of Light celestially dignified by degree and office in general and particular Every and each one for and by itself respectively appertaining to your hierarchy mansion or place of residence to visible appearance move therefore O you benevolent Intelligence* **Graphiel** *with all others of your order office hierarchy or mansion jointly and severally as aforesaid gird up and gather yourself or selves accordingly together and one or more of you as it shall please God of His special grace and permission is given to you and also accordingly descend from your mansion or place of residence or wheresoever else you may be otherwise officiating chancely absent therefrom and immediately forthwith appear visibly here before us in this crystal stone standing here before us and in and through the same to transmit your true and real presence in splendid appearance plainly unto the sight of our eyes utter your voices unto our ears that we may not only visibly see you but audibly hear and speak unto you and that we may converse with you or otherwise forthwith appear out of them visibly upon this triangle or fairly upon the floor and show plainly and visibly unto us a sufficient sign or test of your coming and appearance therefore we do invocate you and undeniably request you charge constrain command and powerfully move you O you Royal and Amicable Angel or blessed Intelligence* **Graphiel** *who art truly ascribed to the planet Mars and by the great Names of God governing that planet:* **Adonay:**

Melech: Eheiah Jehovah: *I do again and again powerfully without any delay lingering or leaving strictly charge that you defer not one minute longer to serve us and really fulfil all that is appropriate and belonging to your charge under the planet Mars **Graphiel: Graphiel: Graphiel:** gird up move come forth and faithfully answer to all that belong to your Hierarchy office or order I being armed with power from above **Graphiel** behold the Exorcist the saying of the very idea the Microcosm by **Agla: El: On: Tetragrammaton** by **Ogim Osj** who sits upon the throne by all that has been Now is and Ever Shall be by the patriarchs and prophets by the great banner **Shemhamphorash** by heaven earth hell: **Graphiel:** thou blessed Intelligence of Mars by all aforesaid move, move, move come forth and visibly show yourself at this very minute as you will answer the contrary being high misdemeanour at your peril before Him who shall come to judge the quick and the dead and the world by fire, fiat, fiat, fiat, for why we are servants of the same your God and true worshippers of the highest wherefore be friendly unto us and do for us as for the servants of the highest whereunto in his Name we do again earnestly request urgently and undeniably move you both in power and presence O you Royal Spirit **Graphiel** whose friendship unto us herein and works shall be a song of honour and the praise of your God in His Creation Amen.*

Conjuration of Nachiel

*O you Benevolent Intelligence of Celestial Light dignified and by nature Angelic who are known or called by the name **Nachiel** and said to be of the nature and office of the planet or star called Sol or the Sun when by celestial position it shall be both essentially well dignified and fortified with all others your substitute the president Intelligences or dignified powers of Light properly residing in or otherwise appertaining to your mansion order or hierarchy from the Superior to the Inferior and serving the Most High God in your respective orders and office as Mediums of Divine grace and mercy and as in charge commanded and appointed we the servants also of the Highest reverently present in His holy fear do earnestly beseech humbly request strongly invocate call forth and powerfully move you to visible appearance in by and through these Excellent Ineffable Great Signal Sacred and Divine Names of your God: **Eloh: El Elo ben Jehovah** even the omnipotent Immortal Immense and Incomprehensible and Most High God and Lord of Hosts **Jehovah** before whom the whole choir of heaven continually sings **Omappa Laman Hallelujah** and by the Seal of your Creation being a mark or character of Holiness unto you and by the great mystery virtue force and power efficacy and influence of all we do strongly invocate confidently call forth and powerfully move you O you benevolent Intelligence or angelic Mediums of Light celestially dignified who by name are called **Nachiel** with all others the president and servient Angels or Mediums of Light celestially dignified by degree and office in general and particular every and each one for and by itself respectively appertaining to your hierarchy mansion or place of residence to visible appearance move therefore O you benevolent Intelligence **Nachiel** with all others of your order office hierarchy or mansion jointly and severally as aforesaid gird up and gather yourself or selves accordingly together and one or more of you as it shall please God of his special grace and permission is given to you and also accordingly descend from your mansion or place of residence or wheresoever else you may be otherwise officiating chancely absent therefrom and immediately forthwith appear visibly here before us in this crystal stone standing here before us and through the same to transmit your true and real presence in splendid appearance plainly unto the sight of our eyes utter your voices unto our ears that we may not only visibly see you but audibly hear you speak unto us and that we may converse with you or otherwise forthwith appear out of them visibly upon this triangle or fairly upon the floor and show plainly and visibly unto us a sufficient sign or test of your coming and appearance therefore we do entreat you and undeniably request you charge constrain command and powerfully move you O you Royal & Amicable Angel or Blessed Intelligence **Nachiel** who art truly ascribed to the planet Sol or the Sun and by the great Names of God governing that planet **Eloh El Elo ben***

Jehovah *I do again and again powerfully without any delay lingering or leaving strictly charge that you defer not one minute longer to serve us and really fulfil all that is appropriated and belonging to your charge under the planet Sol or the Sun **Nachiel: Nachiel: Nachiel:** gird up move and come forth and faithfully answer to all that belongs to your Hierarchy office or order I being armed with power from Above,* ***Nachiel*** *behold the Exorcist the stamp of the very Idea the Microcosm by:* ***Eloh: El Eloben*** *by* ***Ogim Osj*** *who sits upon the Throne by all that has been Now is and Ever Shall be by the patriarchs and prophets by the great Banner* ***Shemhamphorash*** *by heaven Earth & hell* ***Nachiel*** *thou blessed Intelligence of Sol or the Sun by all aforesaid Move Move Move come forth and visibly show yourself at this very minute as you will answer the contrary being high misdemeanour at your peril before Him Who Shall Come to Judge the quick and the Dead and the world by fire: fiat: fiat: fiat: for why we are Servants of the Same your God and true Worshippers of the Highest wherefore be friendly unto us and do for us as for the servants of the highest whereunto in his Name we do again earnestly request urgently and undeniably move you both in power and presence O you Royal Spirit* ***Nachiel*** *whose friendship unto us herein and works shall be a song of honour and the praise of your God in His Creation Amen.*

Conjuration of Hagiel

O you Benevolent Intelligence of Celestial Light dignified and by nature Angelic who are known or called by the name **Hagiel** *and said to be of the nature and office of the planet or star called Venus when by celestial position it shall be both essentially well dignified and fortified with all others your substitute the president Intelligences or dignified powers of Light properly residing in or otherwise appertaining to your mansion orders hierarchy from the Superior to the Inferior and serving the Most High God in your respective orders and office as Mediums of Divine Grace and Mercy and as in charge commanded and appointed we the servants also of the Highest reverently present in holy fear do earnestly beseech humbly request strongly invocate call forth and powerfully move you to visible appearance in by and through these excellent ineffable great signal sacred and divine names of your God* **Saday: Dagael** *Even the Omnipotent Immortal Immense Incomprehensible and Most High God and Lord of Hosts* **Jehovah** *before whom the whole choir of heaven continually sings* **Omappa Laman Hallelujah** *and by the Seal of your Creation being the Mark or Character of holiness unto you and by the great mystery virtue force and power efficacy and influence of all we do strongly invocate confidently call forth and powerfully move you O you Benevolent Intelligence or Angelic Mediums of Light celestially dignified who by name are called* **Hagiel** *with all others the president and servient Angels or Mediums of Light Celestially dignified by degree and office in general and particular every and each one for and by itself respectively appertaining to your hierarchy mansion or place of residence to visible appearance move therefore O you Benevolent Intelligence* **Hagiel** *with all others of your order office hierarchy or mansion jointly and severally as aforesaid gird up and gather yourself or selves accordingly together and one or more of you as it shall please God of His special grace and permission is given to you and also accordingly descend from your mansion or place of residence or wheresoever else you may be otherwise officiating or chancely absent therefrom and immediately forthwith appear visibly here before us in this crystal stone standing here before us and in and through the same to transmit your true and real presence in splendid appearance plainly unto the sight of our eyes and your voices unto our ears that we may visibly see you and audibly hear you speak unto us and that we may converse with or otherwise forthwith appear out of them visibly upon this triangle or fairly upon the floor and show plainly and visibly unto us a sufficient sign or test of your coming and appearance therefore we do entreat you and undeniably request you charge constrain command and powerfully move O you Royal and Amicable Angel or Blessed Intelligence* **Hagiel** *who are truly ascribed to the planet Venus and by the great Names of God governing that planet* **Saday: Dagael: Jehovah** *I do again and again powerfully without any delay lingering or* *leaving strictly charge that you defer not one minute longer to serve us and really fulfil all that is appropriate and belonging to your charge under the planet Venus* **Hagiel: Hagiel: Hagiel** *gird up move come forth and faithfully answer to all that belongs to your hierarchy office or order I being armed with power from above* **Hagiel** *behold the Exorcist the Stamp of the very Idea the Microcosm by:* **Saday: Dagael** *by* **Ogim Osj** *who sits upon the Throne by all that has been Now is and Ever Shall be by the patriarchs and prophets by the great Banner* **Shemhamphorash** *by heaven earth hell* **Hagiel** *thou Blessed Intelligence of Venus by all aforesaid Move, Move, Move come forth and visibly show yourself at this very minute as you will answer the contrary being high misdemeanour at your peril before Him who shall come to judge the quick and the dead and the World by fire fiat fiat fiat for why we are servants of the same your God and true worshippers of the Highest wherefore be friendly unto us and do for us as for the servants of the Highest wherefore in his Name we do again earnestly request urgently and undeniably move you both in power and presence O you Royal Spirit* **Hagiel** *whose friendship unto us herein and works shall be a song of honour & the praise of your God in His Creation Amen.*

Conjuration of Tiriel

O you Benevolent Intelligence of Celestial Light Dignified and by Nature Angelic who are known or called by the name **Tiriel** *and said to be of the nature and office of the planet or star called Mercury when by celestial position it shall be both essentially well dignified and fortified with all others your substitute the president Intelligences or dignified powers of Light properly belonging residing in or otherwise appertaining to your mansion orders hierarchy from the Superior to the Inferior and serving the Most High God in your respective orders and office as mediums of divine grace and mercy and as in charge commanded and appointed we the servants also of the Highest reverently here present in His holy fear do earnestly beseech humbly request strongly invocate call forth and powerfully move you to visible appearance in by and through these excellent sacred and divine names of your God* **Din: Doni: Asboga:**[109] *even the Omnipotent Immortal Immense Incomprehensible and Most High God and Lord of Hosts* **Jehovah** *before whom the whole choir of heaven continually sings* **Omappa Laman Hallelujah** *and by the Seal of your Creation being the Mark or Character of holiness unto you and by the great mystery virtue force power efficacy and influence of all we do strongly invocate confidently call forth and powerfully move you O you Benevolent Intelligence or Angelic Mediums of Light celestially dignified who by name are called* **Tiriel** *with all others the president and servient Angels or Mediums of Light celestially dignified by degree and office in general and particular every and each one for and by itself respectively appertaining to your hierarchy mansion or place of residence to visible appearance move therefore O you Benevolent Intelligence* **Tiriel** *with all others of your orders office hierarchy or mansion jointly and severally as aforesaid gird up and gather yourself or selves accordingly together and one or more of you as it shall please God of His special grace and permission is given to you and also accordingly descend from your mansion or place of residence or wheresoever else you may be otherwise officiating or chancely absent therefrom and immediately forthwith appear visibly here before us in this crystal stone standing here before us and through the same to transmit your true and real presence in splendid appearance plainly unto the sight of our eyes utter your voices unto our ears that we may not only visibly see you but audibly hear you speak unto us and that we may converse with or otherwise forthwith appear out of them visibly upon this triangle or fairly upon the floor and show plainly and visibly unto us a sufficient sign or test of your coming and appearance therefore we do entreat you and undeniably request you charge constrain command and powerfully move you O you Royal Intelligence* **Tiriel** *who are truly ascribed to the planet Mercury and by the*

---

109 Divine names given for the Mercury kamea.

*great Names of God governing that planet **Din Doni Asboga** I do again and again powerfully without any delay lingering or leaving strictly charge that you defer not one minute longer to serve us and really fulfil all that is appropriate and belonging to your charge under the planet Mercury **Tiriel Tiriel Tiriel** gird up move and come forth faithfully answer to all that belongs to your hierarchy office or order I being armed with power from above **Tiriel** behold the Exorcist the Stamp of the very Idea the Microcosm by: **Din: Doni: Asboga** by **Ogim Osj** who sits upon the throne by all that has been Now is and Ever Shall be by the patriarchs and prophets by the great Banner **Shemhamphorash** by heaven earth and hell **Tiriel** thou blessed Intelligence of Mercury by all aforesaid Move, Move, Move come forth and visibly show yourself at this very minute as you will answer the contrary being high misdemeanour at your peril before Him who shall come to judge the quick and the dead and the world by fire fiat fiat fiat for why we are servants of the same your God and true Worshippers of the highest wherefore be friendly unto us and do for us as for the servants of the Highest whereunto in His name we do again earnestly request urgently and undeniably move you both in power and presence O you Royal Spirit **Tiriel** whose friendship unto us herein and works shall be a song of honour and the praise of your God in your Creation Amen.*

Conjuration of Malcha

*O you benevolent Intelligence of celestial light dignified and by Nature Angelic who are known or called by the name **Malcha** and said to be of the nature and office of the planet or star called Luna or the Moon when by celestial position it shall be both essentially well dignified and fortified with all others your substitute the president Intelligences or dignified powers of Light properly belonging Residing in or otherwise appertaining to your mansion orders hierarchy from the Superior to the Inferior and serving the Most High God in your respective orders and office as mediums of divine grace and mercy and as in charge commanded and appointed we the servants also of the Highest reverently here present in holy fear do earnestly beseech humbly request strongly invocate call forth and powerfully move you to visible appearance in by and through these excellent ineffable great signal sacred and divine names of your God **Hod Elem Elojah** the Omnipotent Immortal Immense Incomprehensible and Most High God and Lord of Hosts **Jehovah** before whom the whole choir of heaven continually sings **Omappa Laman Hallelujah** by the Seal of your Creation being the Mark or Character of holiness unto and by the great mystery virtue force and power efficacy and influence of all we do strongly invocate confidently call forth and powerfully move you O you Benevolent Intelligence or Angelic Mediums of Light celestially dignified who by name are called **Malcha** with all others the president and servient Angels or Mediums of Light celestially dignified by degree and office in general and particularly appertaining to your hierarchy mansion or place of residence to visible appearance move therefore O you benevolent Intelligence **Malcha** with all others of your orders office hierarchy or mansion jointly and severally as aforesaid gird up and come away gather yourself or selves accordingly together and one or more of you as it shall please God of His special favour grace and permission is given to you and also accordingly descend from your mansion or place of residence or wheresoever else you may be otherwise officiating or chancely absent therefrom and immediately forthwith appear visibly here before us in this crystal stone standing here before us and through the same to transmit your true and real presence in splendid appearance plainly unto our sight of our eyes utter your voices unto our ears that we may not only visibly see you but audibly hear you speak unto us and that we may converse with you or otherwise forthwith appear out of the same visibly upon this triangle or fairly upon the floor and show plainly and visible unto us a sufficient sign or test of your coming and appearance therefore we do entreat you and undeniably request you charge constrain command and powerfully move you O you Royal Intelligence **Malcha** who are truly ascribed to the planet Luna or the Moon and by the great Names of God governing the planet **Hod Elem Elojah** I do again and again powerfully without delay lingering or leaving strictly charge that you defer not* one minute longer to serve us and really fulfil all that is appropriated and belonging to your charge under the planet Luna or the Moon **Malcha: Malcha: Malcha:** gird up move and come forth faithfully answer to all that belongs to your hierarchy office or order I being armed with power from above **Malcha** behold the Exorcist the Stamp of the very Idea the Microcosm by: **Hod Elem Elojah** by **Ogim Osj** who sits upon the throne all that has been Now is and Ever Shall be by the patriarchs and prophets by the great banner **Shemhamphorash** by heaven earth hell **Malcha** thou blessed Intelligence of Luna by all aforesaid Move, Move, Move come forth and visibly show yourself at this very minute as you will answer the contrary being high misdemeanour at your peril before Him who shall come to judge the quick and the dead and the world by fire fiat fiat fiat for why we are servants of the same your God and true worshippers of the Highest wherefore be friendly unto us and Do for us as for the Servants of the highest whereunto in his Name we do again earnestly request urgently and undeniably move you both in power and presence O you Royal Spirit **Malcha** whose friendship unto us herein and works shall be a song of honour and the praise of your God in Creation Amen.

APPENDIX VII: Shapes of Spirits

The *Fourth Book of Occult Philosophy*, which may have been written in part by Cornelius Agrippa (opinions on this differ) includes a section on the shapes of the familiar spirits of the planets, included here for examples of possible forms the Planetary Intelligences or their servants may appear in. It should be noted that this list is not specifically about the Intelligences and so is here as a guide. For example during a conjuration of Nachiel he appeared as a large black panther with golden wings like lightning and fiery eyes.

The earlier *Sworn Book of Honorius* (SBH) also gives descriptions of planetary spirits, which I have also included for the same reason.

Saturn	Includes a King with a beard seen riding on a Dragon, an old man with a beard, an old woman leaning on a staff, a hog, a Dragon, an owl, a black garment, a hook or sickle or as a Juniper tree. SBH: long and slender bodies, pale or yellow.
Jupiter	A man wearing a mitre in a long robe, a maid with a laurel crown, adorned with flowers, a bull, stag or peacock. It may also manifest as a sword, a box tree or as an azure coloured garment. SBH: medium stature, colour like sky or crystal.
Mars	Includes symbols such as weapons, the wolf and the colour red. Spirits associated with Mars may also appear as an armed King riding upon a wolf, an armed man, a woman holding a buckler on her thigh, a goat, a horse, a stag, wool or as red garments. SBH: bodies of medium stature, dry and thin, colour is red.
The Sun	A King with a sceptre riding on a lion, a crowned King, a Queen with a sceptre, a bird, a lion, a cock, a yellow or golden garment and a sceptre. SBH: bodies are great and large and full of benevolence, the colours are bright or citrus, like gold.

Venus	Images of the beautifully dressed and clothed maid (Venus), A King with a sceptre riding upon a camel, a She-Goat, Camel or Dove. Flowers and garments in the colours white or green are also often cited. SBH: bodies of medium stature in all ways, neither small nor large, fat nor thin, form is agreeable and white as snow.
Mercury	Classic Mercurial symbols such as the fair youth (Hermes or Mercury), the magpie and a robe of changeable colours. Other manifestations described are a King riding upon a bear, a woman holding a distaff, a dog, a she bear, a rod and a little staff. SBH: forms are changeable, clear like glass or like a flame of white fire.
The Moon	Classical image of a female huntress with a bow and arrows (Artemis/Diana), as well as the arrow itself and the colour silver. Lunar spirits may also appear as a King riding on a Doe, a little boy, a cow, a little doe, a goose, a creature with many feet or in the form of green or silver coloured garments. SBH: bodies are long and large, forms are dark and white like crystal or a burnished sword, or like ice or dark clouds.

Appendix VIII: Dream Charms

THIS TECHNIQUE is found in *The Secret of Secrets*,[110] a sixteenth century grimoire owned by several cunning-folk. It involves the creation of a charm which is placed under the pillow prior to sleeping.

The person using the charm should not eat supper, and should burn an appropriate planetary resin in the bedroom before going to sleep. As the charm is placed under the pillow, say:

O holy, glorious, wise, omnipotent God of all secrets, through virtue of this figure show you to me [N] such things in my sleep [as will aid my contact with Planetary Intelligence name].[111]

The charm is created by drawing the kamea on a rectangle, but leaving space around the top and two sides (see following page). Above the kamea are written the name of the Intelligence, the Seal of the Planet ,and the Sigil of the Intelligence.[112] There are some corrupted symbols on the left-hand side of the original, but I have excluded these. As Tiriel was the one given in the manuscript I have included it, but any of the others can easily be reproduced in the same style.

---

110 Published as *A Cunning Man's Grimoire*, 2018.

111 The latter part in square brackets has been added by me to the original which precedes it, as the purpose is to encourage contact with the Planetary Intelligence you are working with.

112 As the original uses the Agrippa version of the sigil I have included it here.

TIRIEL							
8	58	59	5	4	62	63	1
49	15	14	52	53	11	10	56
41	23	22	44	46	19	18	45
32	34	36	29	25	38	39	28
40	26	27	37	36	30	31	33
17	47	46	20	21	43	42	24
9	55	54	12	13	51	50	16
64	2	3	61	60	6	7	57

BIBLIOGRAPHY

Agrippa, Cornelius & Purdue, Eric (ed, trans) (2021) *Three Books of Occult Philosophy*. Rochester. Inner Traditions.

DuQuette, Lon Milo (1999) *My Life With The Spirits: The Adventures of a Modern Magician*. Weiser.

Klaasen, Frank (ed) (2019) *Making Magic in Elizabethan England: Two Early Modern Vernacular Books of Magic*. Pennsylvania: Penn State University Press.

Lucentini, Paolo & Compagni, Vittoria Perrone (eds) (2006) 'Hermetic Literature II, Latin Middle Ages,' in *Dictionary of Gnosis & Western Esotericism*, Hanegraaff, Wouter J. (ed). Leiden. Brill.

MacDonald, Michael Albion (ed & trans) (1988) *De Nigromancia [attributed to] Roger Bacon*. New Jersey. Heptangle Books

Miller, Jason (2022) *Consorting with Spirits. Your Guide to Working with Invisible Allies*. York Beach. Weiser Books.

Ortiz, Nicolás Álvarez (2018) *The Key of Necromancy*. Volume 1. Mexico. Enodia Press.

Peterson, Joseph H. (ed) (2021) *Elucidation of Necromancy*. Lake Worth. Ibis Press.

Peterson, Joseph H. (ed) (2016) *The Sworn Book of Honorius*. Lake Worth. Ibis Press.

Peterson, Joseph H. (ed, trans) (2007) *Grimorium Verum*. CreateSpace.

Proclus & Dodds, E.R. (ed) (1963) *The Elements of Theology*. Oxford. Oxford University Press.

Rankine, David (2023) *The Grimoire Encyclopaedia* (2 vols). Keighley. Hadean Press

Rankine, David (2021) *Climbing the Tree of Life*. Glastonbury. Avalonia.

Rankine, David (2019) *Conjuring the Planetary Intelligences*. Keighley. Hadean Press.

Rankine, David (ed) (2009) *The Book of Treasure Spirits*. London. Avalonia.

Rankine, David (ed) (2009) *A Collection of Magical Secrets*. London. Avalonia

Rankine, David (2009) *Agrippa and the Magic Squares*, in *Howlings*. Dover. Scarlet Imprint

Rankine, David & d'Este, Sorita (2008) *Practical Elemental Magick*. London. Avalonia.

Rankine, David & d'Este, Sorita (2007) *Practical Planetary Magick*. London. Avalonia.

Skinner, Stephen & Rankine, David (2018) *A Cunning Man's Grimoire*. London. Golden Hoard

Skinner, Stephen & Rankine, David (2008) *The Veritable Key of Solomon*. London. Golden Hoard.

Skinner, Stephen & Rankine, David (2007) *The Goetia of Dr Rudd*. London. Golden Hoard.

Skinner, Stephen & Rankine, David (2005) *The Keys to the Gateway of Magic*. London. Golden Hoard.

Skinner, Stephen (2021) *Techniques of Solomonic Magic*. Singapore: Golden Hoard Press.

INDEX

A

A Cunning Man's Grimoire 5
Agiel 7
Agrippa, Heinrich Cornelius 2, 5, 6, 10, 11, 28, 40
altar 13, 14, 19, 24

B

banishing 36, 49, 51
black-handled knife 22
book ii, v, 1, 2, 13, 15, 16, 39
Boxgrove Manual 3, 5, 25
burin 16

C

candles 23, 24, 34, 35
censer 17, 35
circle 13-14, 21-22
  activation 11
  consecration 2
confession 33, 34
Conjuring the Planetary Intelligences. *See* Sloane 3821
conjuror 1, 13, 21, 22, 45, 46, 47, 48, 49, 50
Consecration of
  Candles (and Taper) 23
  Charcoal Blocks 26
  Glasses/Contact Lenses 26
  Holy Water 25
  Incense 24
  Ink/Paint 24
  Jewelry 26
  Miscellaneous Items 17, 27
  Oil 25
  Paper/Parchment 25
  Ring 19

Book 15
Burin 16
Censer/Oil Burner 17
Crystal 18
Pen 19
Ring 19
Robe 20
Silk Cloth 21
Sword 22
crystal 18, 34
  ball 17

E

elemental theory 39

F

fasting 30-31
  electronic fast 31

G

Goetia 38, 74, 104
Graphiel 8
Grimoire of Pope Honorius 5
grimoire practice 2, 3, 14
Grimorium Verum 5, 52, 103

H

Hagiel 5, 9
holy oil 13, 17, 20, 23, 27, 29, 47

I

incense 13, 14, 15, 24, 28, 34
Intelligences
  description of 5–6
  history of 6–7
  qualities of 7–10

J

Johphiel. *See* Jophiel
Jophiel 7

K

kamea 5, 35, 50
Key of Solomon 2, 5, 16, 18, 19, 20, 21, 22, 23, 24, 25, 26, 32, 33, 48
license to depart 50

M

magical momentum 5, 12, 13, 14, 31, 32
magic circle 11, 13, 14, 18, 21, 36, 42, 45, 46, 50
  permanent 43
  portable 43
Malcha 5, 10
Malcha Betarsisim. *See* Malcha
materia magica 23
mirror 17, 34

N

Nachiel 8
Nakhiel. *See* Nachiel

O

obsidian 17
oil burner 17, 35
oils 13, 28, 29
  essential 13, 14, 28, 29, 32, 34, 35, 45

P

pen 18, 19, 35
Pentacle of Solomon 15
planetary aspects 12
planetary hour 11, 15, 30, 42
planetary relationships 11–12
planning 52
Pneumatologia Occulta 5

prayer 15, 16, 30, 33, 46, 48, 49, 52
preparation 5, 13, 30, 32, 52
Proclus 6, 7
purification 13, 30, 32, 52
  baths 31

R

ring 19
robe 20

S

scribe 1, 22, 46, 49
sequence of a conjuration 45
silk cloth 21
skryer 1, 5, 13, 17, 39, 45, 46, 47, 48, 49
Sloane 3821 5, 6, 7, 8, 9
solitary practice 1
sword 21, 22, 34

T

The Magus 5
Three Books of Occult Philosophy 5, 28
Tiriel 5, 9
triangle 17, 22, 34, 38, 39, 40, 41, 45, 47, 48, 50

www.ingramcontent.com/pod-product-compliance
Lightning Source LLC
Chambersburg PA
CBHW071512150426
43191CB00009B/1501